T   F

THIRD REICH
AT WAR

MIDDLE SCHOOL AND OTHER DISASTERS

Worst Broommate Ever!

BY WANDA COVEN

ILLUSTRATED BY ANNA ABRAMSKAYA

Simon Spotlight

New York London Toronto Sydney New Delhi

SIMON SPOTLIGHT

An imprint of Simon & Schuster Children's Publishing Division

1230 Avenue of the Americas, New York, New York 10020

First Simon Spotlight edition May 2023

Copyright © 2023 by Simon & Schuster, Inc.

All rights reserved, including the right of reproduction in whole or in part in any form.

SIMON SPOTLIGHT and colophon are registered trademarks of Simon & Schuster, Inc.

For information about special discounts for bulk purchases, please contact Simon & Schuster Special Sales at 1-866-506-1949 or business@simonandschuster.com. The Simon & Schuster Speakers Bureau can bring authors to your live event. For more information or to book an event contact the Simon & Schuster Speakers Bureau at 1-866-248-3049 or visit our website at www.simonspeakers.com.

Text by Alison Inches

Series designed by Chani Yammer, based on the Heidi Heckelbeck series designed by Aviva Shur

Cover designed by Laura Roode

Illustrated by Anna Abramskaya, inspired by the original character designs of Priscilla Burris from the Heidi Heckelbeck chapter book series

The illustrations for this book were rendered with digital ink and a bunch of love.

The text of this book was set in Minou.

Manufactured in the United States of America 0423 FFG

10 9 8 7 6 5 4 3 2 1

Library of Congress Control Number 2022936494

ISBN 978-1-6659-2528-0

ISBN 978-1-6659-2529-7 (ebook)

To my readers:
You are magical.
Love,

Wanda

GOODBYE, BREWSTER!

Okay, here we go.

I, Heidi Heckelbeck, am officially freaking out, so I hurl myself onto my bed.

AAHHH!!
Totally freaking out here!

Flump!

I bury my face in my pillow.

Please don't let boarding school be super, totally, and utterly horrible, I think.

Then I wonder:

Why in the world did I agree to go anyway?

I mean, sure, I definitely want to become a better witch, and yes, I'll put on a brave face, but I'm not gonna lie, **I'm terrified of living away from home.**

This is a life-changing step.

I roll over and grab a framed picture of **my two best friends, Lucy and Bruce.**

There I am, standing in the middle, with one arm around each of them.

We look so happy by the pool!

This picture is definitely going with me— even though the sight of it tugs at my heart, and even though I hardly have any room left in my suitcases!

My door creaks open.

"Heidi?" Mom walks in with a stack of white towels. "Honey, what are you doing? We need to hit the road in *less* than an hour."

I push myself up to sitting and twist my hair into a messy bun.

"I'm having a *moment.*"

Mom sets the towels on the bed beside me. "Well, it's totally natural to feel anxious before leaving for boarding school. To be honest, I was petrified."

It comforts me to know Mom was scared too.

"It's just that I'm going to miss everyone SO much."

Mom rests her hand on my shoulder.

"Remember, your friends and family will *always* be here. And now you get to make *more* friends."

She gives me a smile before continuing.

"It'll be an adventure! The rest of us will be missing *you* more than you'll be missing us. And you'll love Broomsfield Academy—just like Aunt Trudy and I did. *I promise.*"

I press the picture of my friends against my chest. Mom points to my duffel bags. "Now, time to finish packing."

I drop to my knees beside my new comforter, neatly folded inside a see-through plastic case.

This comforter is totally *me.*

It has ribbons of patchwork, with spirals, paisley, polka dots, and itty-bitty flowers. The other side has navy-and-white stripes. Navy pom-poms dangle from the edges. It'll look SO good on my bed at school. This makes me feel a smidge better.

Mom nudges me again.

Okay, okay.

I grab the towels and begin to shove them into an empty duffel bag.

"Tell me more about Broomsfield Academy." Mom's already told me about it a bazillion times, but it helps to talk about it.

"Well, as you know, it's the only school in the country that has secret classes for witches-in-training."

I sigh dreamily.

"I know! I wish I could take magic classes ALL day *every* day."

Mom laughs. "Well, you have to take *regular* classes like English, math, and science too."

I like all those subjects, but **wouldn't they be way more fun if they had a bit more magic in them?**

Like, what if I could enchant my books so the story would come to life in the classroom?

Or what if I could magically solve climate change in science class?

And I would definitely be psyched if my pencil could take notes all by itself! Think about it. No more cramped fingers or eraser dust!

Mom hands me a stack of sheets to pack with my towels, totally interrupting my thoughts.

She knows the way my mind works.

"Slow down, Li'l Miss Witch," she says. "Remember that ALL Broomsfield witches and wizards are **sworn to secrecy.**"

She puts a hand on my mine, and I turn to look at her. She locks eyes with me and continues.

"Heidi, absolutely none of the other students can find out about the School of Magic program. That's **the beauty of Broomsfield Academy.** The classes for magical students are hidden in what seems like a regular, run-of-the-mill boarding school. It's been this way for generations, and anyone who isn't a witch or wizard is none the wiser."

My mom *always* stresses this point.

It's like she thinks I'll be the ONE witch in the school's 150-year history to spill the beans!

Not a chance.

I LOVE secrets!

And I've never given away my own witch identity in all my life, so why would I start NOW?

Mom zips one of my suitcases. "And more important, you're not supposed to practice magic *outside* class," she adds as if I didn't know.

Blah, blah, blah, I say in my head, trying to block out this information.

But the truth is, not practicing magic when I feel like it will be superhard for me.

I *love* to practice magic!

It comes in handy every day, and you can do so
many cool things with magic, like clean your room
without lifting a finger, make random stuff
glow in the dark, or make a pencil bend like
a wet noodle.

And how am I going to change my nail polish every morning, like I do now? And there's no way I can do my hair without magic.

I would never survive without my tangle-tamer and de-frizzing spells!

Okay, I'm seriously getting worked up about this no-magic rule.

Maybe I'll be able to sneak a little *everyday* magic in when nobody's looking—stuff nobody would suspect. . . .

I can be a very clever witch when I want to be. . . .

I look up and notice that Mom has a very stern look on her face. I'm pretty sure she

knows what I'm thinking, so I quickly change
the subject.

"ANYWAY," I say a tad dramatically so I can move
on to my next question. "What will I learn in my
School of Magic classes?"

Mom wheels another suitcase into the hall and
comes back to pack my bathroom stuff.

"Well, for one thing, you'll learn the history of
magic."

Makes sense, but I want to learn new spells.
I want to be able to make my scooter
fly or travel to faraway places with a
blink of my eyes.

"What else?" I ask.

Mom packs a green loofah and a pair of black-and-
white-striped flip-flops for the shower.

"You'll learn how to brew potions and cast
charms and spells, as well as learn the
magical properties of plants and herbs," Mom
goes on. "You'll also learn how to use a
wand."

Now, that's what I'm talking about!

I squeal as I shove a neatly folded pillowcase into
my bag.

I've never used a wand before.

"Hey, how come you never use a wand or practice magic at home?"

This is something I've always wondered about my mom.

"You know *very* well, Heidi. It's because I chose to be a *regular* mom. But that doesn't mean I don't use magic. I'm just discreet about it, and I learned *that* at school."

"But Dad makes more potions than *you* do, and he's not even a wizard!"

Mom frowns. "Yes, but *Dad's* potions don't have magical properties."

I shake my head. "Well, I disagree on that! Dad's soda recipes are magically FIZZ-i-licious!"

My dad's kind of famous. Everybody in Brewster knows he's the head of research and development at a soda company called the FIZZ.

"Okay, I see your point." Mom laughs. "But keep packing, kiddo, if you want to get to school before dinner."

I pull my flowery suitcase off the shelf in my closet. **My favorite stuff will go in here.**

First I wrap the picture of my friends and me, along with a picture of my family, in tissue. I tuck them into the bottom of my suitcase.

Next I lay down my treasured *Book of Spells* and my Witches of Westwick medallion, which are in their leather travel case. They're *really* old and belonged to my great-grandmother.

I cover them with my brand-new white jean jacket.

I can't wait to wear this!

I plop a clear zippered bag on top of it. The bag is stuffed with black-and-white-striped tights. These have been my signature look since forever, but who knows if I'll wear them at boarding school.

It may be time to go for a new style.

Right now I'm kind of into my striped sneakers.
Next I plop two large bags of gummy bears into
my suitcase for my secret stash. Then I place
down a package of *compliment* pencils that
Lucy gave me. One of the pencils says **YOU'RE
MAGICAL**. I smile because Lucy still doesn't even
know I'm a witch! And last but not least, I pack
my new shaving kit because everyone knows girls
shave their legs in middle school.

Duh.

Oh, I almost forgot my comics, word searches, and magazines! I drop them into my suitcase, zip it, and wheel it into the hall.

Then I stare at all my luggage.

Gulp! I'm actually totally packed and ready to go!

Butterflies flutter in my stomach.

Then *WHAM!* Henry's door slams shut.

I nearly jump out of my shoes.

My brother stands in the hall and looks at my bags and then at me.

"Well, I'm not sure what's weirder—having you around or NOT having you around."

My tongue rolls out like a party horn. It's an automatic reflex. Henry points both index fingers at me and makes a silly face.

"Just KIDDING!" he says. "I'm totally going to miss you! The only upside is I'll have all the cereal to myself!"

I retract my tongue. Oh wow, I'll miss racing through boxes of cereal with Henry or fishing for all the yummiest pieces before he wakes up.

I wonder if they'll have cereal at boarding school?

I sure hope so!

"I'll miss you too, bub."

Henry and I each grab a suitcase and roll it downstairs.

Bonk,

bonk,

bonk!

Mom and Dad help with the other suitcases, duffel bags, comforter, fan, and desk lamp.

I race back into the house for one more thing.

It's something I've been working on my *entire* life.

I call it my Thingamajiggy and Whatnot Collection.

Inside this giant plastic storage tub **is every single prize I have ever gotten** from a gumball machine, trick-or-treating, or fast-food kid's meal— plus everything from all my birthday party goody bags.

Truth moment here.

I have never thrown even one of these little doodads away.

I have everything in here from animal erasers and Mr. Potato Head parts, to Kool-Aid packets and miniature plastic foods—even leftover Halloween candy.

This miscellaneous stuff comes in handy for spells. You never know when you might need some weird trinket in a potion or mix.

It happens A LOT.

I plunk my tub full of treasures in the driveway with my other stuff, and Dad loads everything into the car. Henry and I hop into the back seat.

The butterflies in my stomach are really flapping now.

I take one long last look at our house. Home sweet home. I'm going to miss it so much.

"Farewell, house! I love you!"

I say this as Dad backs down the driveway.

We're not even to the end of the driveway when a car pulls up.

It's my absolute best friend in the whole world, LUCY!

She already threw me a going-away party with all our friends, but here she is to say one last goodbye! Dad stops the car, and I hop out.

Lucy and I run to each other and hug like koalas. She has a purple shopping bag in her hand.

What's in there? I wonder. Lucy pulls out a scrapbook.

"I finally finished it! It's a scrapbook filled with everything about *us* since second grade." She hands it to me. At the same time, my knees suddenly feel all wobbly, like Jell-O.

The thought of leaving Lucy hits me like a freight train.

Tears fill my eyes.

We grab hold of each other again.

"Thank you SO much," I manage to say. "I'm going to miss you more than all the Skittles in Skittlesville!"

Lucy pulls away so we can see each other face-to-face.

"Me too," she says. Her eyes also glisten with tears.

"What am I going to do without you?" I sniffle and laugh at the same time. "Maybe you and Melanie will become BFFs . . . !"

Lucy laughs so hard, she snorts. "I seriously doubt it! You're so lucky to be rid of her!"

I can't help but start laughing too. "All good things must come to an end!"

Then we hug one more time.

"This isn't really goodbye," I say. "I'll come home on weekends sometimes. And there are phone calls and texting and letters."

Lucy nods. "I know. Love you forever."

"Me too."

Lucy runs back to her car.

I wave at Mrs. Lancaster.

Then I run back to our car and plop onto the back seat.

I glance at the scrapbook in my hands. The cover has a photo of me and Lucy. It was one of our first photos together, from when we were both about seven years old.

I can't look at it right now, or I'll go to pieces.

As our car rolls down our street, I watch the familiar scene disappear behind me.

"Goodbye, neighborhood!

"Goodbye, friends!

"Goodbye, life as I know it!"

Then Henry looks up from his tablet with one eyebrow raised.

"Adios, DRAMA QUEEN!"

I shove Henry. He shoves me right back. Then I roll down my window.

"Goodbye, Brewster!" I roll it back up. "And look out, magical new world! Because . . .

"HERE I COME!"

Then, with a tiny bit of magic, I make the leaves in our driveway swirl around and form the word

"goodbye." I don't even have to mix a spell to move things anymore. But *uh-oh*, Mom saw what I just did. *Oops.*

"HEIDI!" she says as she turns around and glares at me.

"Okay, okay!" I say, and I make the leaves swirl randomly again. Hey, can't a budding witch have a little fun?!

HELLO, BROOMSFIELD!

We've only been driving fifteen minutes, and we're already in the countryside.

Seriously!

We're surrounded by cornfields, cows, horses, and red barns.

Who knew the boonies were less than an hour away?

Broomsfield is even more rustic because it's a *whole* hour away. The roads are squiggly, like cooked spaghetti, and the houses have Christmas lights that stay up year-round.

Three words: *merry* and *weird.*

"Hey, Henry! We're passing a cemetery! Hold your breath!"

Henry and I each take a huge gulp of air at the same time. With puffed cheeks we pass the cemetery. We've done this since we were little.

One word: *tradition.*

When we get to Harvey's Hat Museum, we exhale dramatically.

Whoever heard of a HAT museum anyway?

And why are there zany tourist attractions in the countryside?

This reminds me of this kooky park and zoo we used to go to when we were little.

"Remember Happy Hollow?" I say to everyone in the car.

Somehow it comforts me to reminisce about childhood right now.

It makes me feel happy and safe.

Henry laughs.

"How could anyone forget *that* creepy place? Happy Hollow would make a good set for a scary movie."

I totally agree with Henry.

All the rides at Happy Hollow were at least fifty years old.

It was like stepping back in time.

They even had a weird puppet theater castle and a steep rickety slide inside a gigantic boot. It had something to do with some nursery rhyme about an old woman who lived in a shoe.

Creepers!

Dad flicks on the blinker and turns off the main road. Gravel crunches under the tires as we pull up to a farm stand.

"Pumpkins!" I cry. I *love* pumpkins!

Mom frowns. "It's too early for pumpkins."

"It's *never* too early for pumpkins!"

But it makes me wonder.

Will we get to carve pumpkins at boarding school?

Will they let us go trick-or-treating?

Lucy and I made a promise to go together until we're eighteen. Fingers crossed that Halloween falls on a weekend so Lucy and I can still go trick-or-treating.

I pick out a shiny red McIntosh apple, pay for it, and give it a quick wash at the water pump. If we can't go trick-or-treating, I'll be sadder than sad.

Ugh. Why does it feel like my childhood is coming to an end?

Answer: *because maybe it is. . . .*

I'm just about to bite into my apple when I realize something else weird.

I don't feel like eating.

My stomach is still churning, and I have this funny feeling in my throat.

Okay, I am still officially freaking out about leaving home.

I shove the apple into my backpack for later and climb into the car. Henry is happily munching and playing some squash-the-fruit game on his tablet.

He doesn't have a care in the world.

Lucky.

But I have *so* many cares!

Who will my roommate be?

And what will she be like?

Will we be close friends?

What if we have *zero* in common?

Will my roommate be a witch, like me?

OMGosh, the suspense is torture!

As Mom and Dad come back to the car and we pull away from the farm stand, I text Lucy.

Hey, LuLu!
Am almost to Broomsfield! Feel like I'm gonna barf, but not really. Does that make sense?

I tap send.

Lucy writes back in a heartbeat.

Makes TOTAL sense! This is a HUGE change, Heidi. Miss you so much already.

I thumb a response.

Miss you already too. Please don't forget about me! 😢 ♥

I stare at the moving dots on my screen as she writes back. ⊘ ⊘ ⊘

How could I forget about you, Hecks? Not possible! And you better not forget me either!

Then she sends a bawling-your-eyes-out emoji and a bunch of red hearts. ♥♥♥♥

I shove my phone back into my bag and stare out the window.

Part of me wants to turn around and go home *right now*, but I know that's not really an option.

How can I become the best witch in the world if I go home?

You can do this, Heidi!

And that's when I see the Broomsfield city limits sign.

Welcome to Broomsfield! The town that will sweep you off your feet! Established in 1856.

There's an image of a broom sweeping. It looks like a witch's broom to me, but most people would see it as any old broom **because *most* people think witches aren't real.**

Little do they know!

Mom says the best witches and wizards in the world go to Broomsfield Academy.

I wonder what it will be like to be around witches and wizards from all over the world every day.

At least I won't have to keep my magical identity a *total* secret, like I had to in elementary school. I'll have other witches to talk to at Broomsfield.

This makes me feel a little better.

"Almost there!" Mom says.

OMGosh!

We just turned onto the main road that leads to school.

In less than three minutes

I will arrive at my new life.

The road is lined with maple trees and a ribbon of old stone walls on either side. It looked so pretty when we visited, **but now that I'm here for real**, it looks strange and unfamiliar.

To make matters worse, **it's cloudy.**

Seriously!

It was perfectly sunny when we left Brewster, **and now it's totally gray.** I'm not a fan of gray.

Gray makes everything look doomsday-ish.

Then an interesting thought occurs to me. **Maybe I could be a *day* student instead of a boarder at Broomsfield?**

My family could buy a house nearby until I finish school . . . ?

I decide to voice my brilliant idea.

"Would you guys consider moving to Broomsfield so I can be a day student?"

My idea is met with an unexpected outburst of laughter.

"What's so funny?"

Henry looks up from his game.

"YOU are! You're chickening out *already!*"

I fold my arms because his comment makes me mad.

So what if I'm having a few chicken-y feelings? I feel I must address this.

"For your information, I am NOT chickening out. I just want to make sure I've considered *every one of* my options—that's all."

Mom peers between the seats. "Heidi, boarding is the best part about Broomsfield. Trust me, you're going to love it. You're not even going to want to come home on weekends."

I thump my folded arms against my chest.

I find THAT *hard to believe.*

So now here I sit, surrounded by my own family, in a total state of discomfort.

Merg.

Dad parks the car in front of the main building, which is stone.

Mom says the architecture is called Gothic.

If you ask me, Gothic architecture looks haunted, and the cloudy day doesn't help matters.

A gargoyle sits on either side of the entrance, and they stare down at me.

Am I in a horror movie?

Etched over the main door is the name EMMA CRAWFORD, the woman who founded Broomsfield

Academy. Mom and Aunt Trudy said Emma Crawford started the secret School of Magic.

"We're here!" Dad announces way too cheerily.

Ugh, the time has come to get out of the car, but instead I sit there glued to the seat.

Why does my mouth feel like I ate an entire bag of cotton balls?

I can't swallow, but for some reason, I keep trying.

Gack.

I feel so much older now that I'm going to middle school, and yet I also want to stay in the car, drive home, and have Mom make me hot chocolate.

How can I be feeling grown-up and like a scared little kid all at the same time?

Somehow I force myself to move and make it inside the building. A lady in a silk blouse, a beige skirt, and pearls hands me a bottle of water. *Bless you, kind woman!* She also hands me a campus map and a blue permanent marker. I fill out a name tag and pat the sticky side to my shirt. Then I find out the name of my dorm. I'm in Irma Baileywick. My mom clasps her hands together.

"Aunt Trudy was in Baileywick!"

"Yay," I say without my normal enthusiasm, though I'm very happy to be in Aunt Trudy's old dorm. I love the family connection, and Baileywick is one of the oldest dorms on campus, which is also kind of cool.

"Welcome, Heidi!" says a girl with hazel eyes, wavy chocolate-brown mermaid hair, and a huge cheerleader grin. "My name is Jenna Lopez, and I'm a student here *and* your resident advisor—or 'RA' for short! I'm going to help you move in." She hands me another map.

Jenna rolls a large white canvas cart over to us, and my parents show her to our car. Henry and I follow. Dad beeps open the back of the car, and the door rises, **revealing all my worldly possessions.**

My legs feel wobbly again.

Jenna and Dad load my stuff into the cart,
and I know I should help, but I watch like a
bewildered deer.

Do something! I tell myself.

So I open the car door.

"I'll get my stuff from the back seat," I say, trying
to sound helpful, but it doesn't really matter
because nobody's paying attention anyway.

Henry's taking selfies
with the gargoyles in
front of the school!

Mom is dabbing
her lips with
raspberry lipstick.
She catches my
eye in the rearview
mirror.

"How are you doing, Heidi?" she asks, popping her lipstick into her bag and opening the car door. I wish I could share all the thoughts and concerns inside my head, but I can't.

Everything's happening so fast.

"I'm okay," I say, even though I feel the exact opposite. Mom winks lovingly. Then we gather around Jenna and follow her to the dorm. The wheels on the cart clatter. Raindrops plink onto my face. *Oh great. Now my hair is going to frizz out.*

Merg.

We pass dorms along the way. They have fun
names like Dreamwood, Whistlestop, Crumpsbank,
and Honeysuckle.

Then Jenna stops in front of Baileywick. My dorm
is stone, like Crawford, only minus the gargoyles.
It has iron windows that crank out.

"Welcome to Baileywick!" Jenna says. "We live on the same floor, Heidi, so you can knock on my door anytime you have questions."

I smile at Jenna—or at least I think I do, but I don't even know anymore.

I'm so far inside my head that I'm not sure what my face is doing.

Jenna wheels the cart inside and onto an old elevator.

My family squishes in around the cart.

"Wow, this elevator is *ancient!*" my little brother says. "It's like a giant birdcage."

Jenna slides the accordion door shut. "Yup, it's at least one hundred years old, but it's safe!" Jenna says.

I look out the elevator door and watch the floors
go by.

"We only use it for moving in and out," Jenna says
as she slides the door open on the third floor. Her
voice echoes in the stone hallway.

We rattle past a common area. A bunch of kids are hanging out on the sofas and chairs, looking at their phones.

We clatter down the hallway and stop in front of Room 307.

Well, this is IT! I say to myself.

The moment I've been thinking about all summer.

I'm about to see my room for the first time and meet my roommate—or I should say "broommate" because that's what roommates are called at Broomsfield Academy.

I squeeze my eyes shut as the door swings in. Then I open them back up. . . .

My jaw drops in shock. . . .

I have to shade my eyes with one hand because . . .

I'm blinded by the color PINK.

My roommate is nowhere in sight, but she's definitely left her mark.

Her stuff is already set up. I quickly analyze her belongings.

Pink comforter with white polka dots—pretty cute.

White lacy dust ruffle. *Uh-oh! I forgot to pack a dust ruffle!* An alarm bell goes off in my head.

Does everyone else here have a dust ruffle?

I'll have to ask Mom to send one.

My broommate also has a fuzzy pink backrest on her bed and two cream heart-shaped pillows. Sweet, but definitely not my style.

Her shower caddy is also pink with white polka dots, and she has a pink loofah. On top of her dresser is a silver tray with tons of moisturizers and perfumes.

She even has a cosmetics suitcase beside her dresser.

One word: *whoa.*

On the wall she has hung a rustic wooden sign that says: YOU ARE A **STAR**. . . . And underneath it says . . . YOU ARE BEAUTIFUL, STRONG, AMAZING, CAPABLE, CONFIDENT, BELOVED.

Above her bed are framed pictures of a giraffe, a zebra, and a llama, all blowing bubble-gum bubbles.

Adorable.

On the floor beside her bed is a round, fuzzy pink rug, and, of course, pink slippers are tucked partway under the bed.

A light box with the letter *M* hangs over her nightstand. This must mean my roommate's name begins with the letter *M*! Instantly I try to guess her name. *Mia? Madison? Macy? Matilda?*

"I'll come back at five forty-five to pick you up for dinner," Jenna says, snapping me out of my thoughts. I nod with relief because I really want to be alone with my family right now.

"Thanks," I say.

Jenna smiles and waves goodbye as she slips out the door with the empty cart.

After she leaves, I size up the room. It's bigger than I thought it would be. The ceilings are tall, and there is a window at the far end. I notice that my roommate has already claimed the bed by the window.

I sort of would have liked to have been consulted on that one, but I guess she got here first.

Also in the room are two desks and two dressers.
There's even a bathroom connected to our room,
which is awesome.

I thought I was going to have to share a community
bathroom in the hall.

Mom pulls out my sheets and comforter, and we
begin to organize my stuff.

I wish we could organize forever
because I really don't want my family
to leave—even Henry.

Why do I feel so clingy?!

"Hey, space cakes!" Henry says, bringing me back to the moment. He bounces onto my freshly made bed and new comforter. I give him the evil eye, but he totally ignores it.

"Your room is SO cool, Heidi! I can't wait till I get to come here!"

It figures that Henry is more chill about going to boarding school than I am right now, but then again, **he gets to go home and sleep in his own bed tonight and hang out with his own friends for the rest of the year.**

"Heidi, where do you want this?" Dad says, holding a hammer and my picture frame with a moon and stars that light up.

I point to a place on the wall.

Dad also hangs my three wooden signs that say: CHILL OUT. DREAM BIG! And YOU'RE MAGICAL.

I place my picture of Lucy, Bruce, and me on my dresser, along with the picture of my family.

Then I hang my clothes, organize my dresser drawers, line up my shoes, and load my shower caddy.

And just like that, I'm unpacked.

"Well, I guess it's time for us to hit the road," Dad says, packing his drill into his tool kit. My family looks at me with puppy-dog eyes.

I force back tears.

"I'll walk you to the car," I say. This time we take the stairs. When we get to the car, Mom and Dad hold out their arms and enfold me into the world's best hug.

"Everything's going to be all right," Mom says. "We'll think about you every single day."

I nod.

Dad pulls me close. "We'll miss having you around, pumpkin."

Henry joins the group hug. "I'm going to miss you so much too. Home won't be the same without you."

And that's when the tears stream down my face.

Mom pulls a tissue from her purse. I sob freely, and it feels weirdly good.

"I'm so lucky to have such an amazing family," I tell them.

Then we say our final goodbyes, and I wave until our car disappears.

And *blammo*—just like that—I'm alone.

I'm feeling two things right now:

Homesick.

And, as my family's car drives farther into the distance, a feeling of excitement starts to build in my stomach where there were only butterflies before.

This is going to be a big adventure, I remind myself.

Let's do this!

SPECIAL GIFTS

I scuff my sneakers on the path back to my dorm.

Campus life buzzes all around me.

Moving bins bumble along the pavement.

A kid laughs and flings a neon Frisbee on the lawn.

It makes me wonder, *How can I jump-start my new social life?*

Magic is the first thing that comes to mind,

but I quickly put that thought away.

I can only use magic if I'm desperate, I tell myself firmly.

But what if I don't fit in?

What if nobody likes me?

I shut down these annoying thoughts too.

I'm only scared because I'm NEW, silly.

And that's when I notice a cute guy with honey-colored bangs and green eyes walking toward me.

"Hi," he says, and smiles.

"Hey," I squeak back in a pixie voice.

Well, THAT sounds pathetic.

I turn and watch him walk away.

He has on khaki shorts and a faded navy T-shirt. He's definitely cute, and it makes me wonder,

Will I have a boyfriend at boarding school?

That would be *so* fun.

I've never had one before—only crushes.

The boys in Brewster are not exactly **electrifying**—probably because I've known them my whole life.

But now I'm at a new school with people from all over the world!

Woo!

Get ready to crush! This is the best I've felt *all* day!

Could he be a wizard?

But then, what if he's not?

How would I explain my being a witch to someone on a date?

"Hi, I'm Heidi. I like chocolate ice cream, gummy bears, and oh, by the way, I have magical powers."

I turn back around so I don't get caught staring at Mr. Cutie Pie.

At the same time, I bump into a girl with long black hair.

Whoops!

I look up and see familiar brown eyes that are breaking into a smile.

Wait a second, *I KNOW this girl!*

"Sunny?" I say in disbelief. The girl's face lights up, like sunshine blazing through a cloud.

"Heidi?" she says, studying my face.

"NO WAY! Is that really YOU?"

I nod and hold out my arms. We give each other a huge, long hug.

I met Sunny at the beach with my family many years ago. Her real name is Sunita Akhtar, but everyone calls her Sunny, **and her personality totally matches her nickname.**

We had the best time at the beach and had kept in touch for many years. We haven't spoken in about a year, though.

Sunny is a witch, like me, and she's the only witch I know outside my own family and the librarian at the Brewster town library.

Now she's the *first* witch I know at Broomsfield!

"Why didn't you call me when you were accepted?" I say.

Sunny shrugs. "I dunno! Probably the same reason you didn't call me when *you* were accepted!" We both laugh. "How did we lose touch anyway?"

"Who knows?" I say. "I'm just SO happy to see you! I should've known you'd be here!"

Sunny grabs my forearms with both hands.

"I'm SO happy to see you too, Heidi! I was feeling pretty homesick after my parents left this afternoon."

I throw my head back and laugh. "Same! My family just left, and I'm still kind of a mess."

We're both laughing now, and it feels so good to see an old friend.

"What dorm are you in?" Sunny asks.

I point in the direction of my dorm. "Baileywick. How about *you*?"

"Honeysuckle. I can see your dorm from my bedroom window."

Sunny shifts her backpack higher onto her shoulder. "Hey, I'm on my way to the campus store. Wanna come? I have to buy toothpaste because I forgot to pack some. Can you believe it? *Duh.*"

I nod knowingly. "I totally get it. And I'd love to go to the store with you! I just need to be back at my dorm by five forty-five."

"No problem!"

Both the student center and the campus store are located in the Barn.

It's called the Barn because it used to be a *real* barn when the school first started.

Back in the old days, the barn was home to over a hundred dairy cows. The cows supplied the school and the town of Broomsfield with milk.

I learned all of this on my campus tour.

The Barn also has two bowling lanes, a movie theater, and a stage.

Hard to believe *cows* used to live there!

As we walk, Sunny and I talk so fast, we stumble over our words.

"Remember those epic sandcastles you used to

build at the beach?" I say. "Your sand kingdoms could've set world records, except for the fact that you used *magic* to build them."

Sunny puts a finger to her lips. *"Shhhh,* be careful, Heidi. We can't let anyone know we're *you-know-whats."*

I cover my mouth with my hand.

"Oops! It's going to be so hard not to talk about *you-know-what* or practice *you-know-what* outside our special classes!"

Sunny leans closer. "Tell me about it!" she whispers. "How has Broomsfield kept the School of Magic a secret for over a hundred years?"

I shake my head. "They probably use a lot of *forgetting* spells."

Then Sunny looks around to make double sure nobody's listening.

"Well, I for one can't wait to start our special classes. There are so many things I want to learn, plus I want to develop my special gift even more."

I raise my eyebrows.

"What do you mean by *special gift*?"

Sunny nudges me with her elbow.

"*You know!* Your special gift as a witch. Every witch has a special gift."

I try not to act surprised, but I have no idea what she's talking about.

Nobody ever told me that *all* witches have a special gift.

Is this really true?

And furthermore, why don't I have a *special gift*?

I panic and quickly turn the topic away from myself. "Um, so what's *your* special gift, Sunny?"

Sunny lifts the pendant from around her neck so I can see it. It's a shimmering sun.

The golden charm looks striking against her brown skin. "Wow, that's so beautiful! What does it mean?"

Sunny puts her pendant back on.

"This sun pendant is a *symbol* of my special gift," she says. "I *use* the sun to perform magic—that's how I made those amazing sandcastles. On a cloudy day, like today, I can't use my special gift. I can only perform spells from my spell book. What about you, Heidi? What's *your* special gift?"

I bite the edge of my lip.

Should I tell Sunny I don't have one?

I guess I'd better fess up.

"I don't have a special gift that I know of. The only thing I can do without my spell book is move objects, but I wouldn't exactly call that a special gift. It's just something I've practiced for a while."

Sunny waves me off, like this is no big deal.

"Don't worry," she says. "I'm sure you'll discover your special gift while you're at Broomsfield. It'll just become obvious."

I nod. Then I disappear back into my head.

I sure hope Sunny is right.

The last thing I'd ever want to be is an average, everyday witch.

Sunny pulls open the door to the Barn. The campus store is right next to the entrance.

Wow, this place has everything! I think as I try to shut out the feeling that I'm missing something major.

I study all the Broomsfield logo stuff—shirts, beanies, loungewear.

Another wall has every snack on the planet. It even has fresh snacks, like yogurt, sandwiches, and cheese-and-cracker trays. *Yum!*

I follow Sunny to the toiletry section. She studies the toothpaste and grabs arctic peppermint. We walk back to the counter, and she charges the toothpaste. Then Sunny leans against the door and holds it open for me.

"Wanna come see my room and meet my roommate, Annabelle?" Sunny asks. "She's from England, and she's a *you-know-what*, like us."

This invitation lightens my mood. "I'd love to!"

"Cool!"

Sunny slides her box of toothpaste into her backpack. "So what's *your* broommate like, Heidi?"

I shrug. "She wasn't there when I arrived. All I know is that her name begins with the letter *M*, she clearly loves the color pink, and she's into spa stuff, *big*-time. I guess I'll meet her soon enough."

Sunny shoves me playfully. "Well, *whoever* she is—she's lucky to have *YOU* for a roommate."

I can't help but smile.

Sunny is so positive!

I follow my friend up the concrete stairs of her dorm.

Honeysuckle is super-modern, with lots of large glass windows. The common area has boxy chairs and sofas with swirly-patterned, bright-colored cushions. It even has giant beanbag chairs in front of the TV.

Some kids are flopped on the beanbags. A few wave as we walk by. Sunny waves back as we jog up a floating staircase. The staircase isn't *really* floating. It just looks like it.

We walk down a white cinder-block hallway with colorful abstract art painted right onto the walls—swishy lines, checkerboards, and spirals.

It's so different from Baileywick.

Sunny opens the door to her room. "We're here!"

I follow her in, and I instantly know which side of the room belongs to Sunny.

Behind her headboard is a bold sunrise made of fabric.

She also has a picture of the sun, moon, and Earth on the wall—not to mention a gorgeous light-up rainbow over her dresser. She even has a sign that says: WHEN YOU CAN'T FIND THE SUNSHINE, **BE** THE SUNSHINE.

It's so upbeat, like Sunny.

The other side of the room is pretty bare, except for a little antique trunk that looks like a treasure chest. There's a girl with chin-length blond hair sitting on the bed. She smiles, and I notice her sparkly blue eyes.

"Meet Annabelle Williams," Sunny says. "Annabelle, this is my old friend Heidi Heckelbeck." Then Sunny leans in and whispers. "Heidi is a witch, like us."

"Hi," Annabelle says. "Please excuse my rather *boring* side of the room. I only brought what I could carry on the plane from England."

I'm enthralled by her bewitching English accent.

Honestly, if she told me to go jump into a lake with *that* accent, I might actually do it.

"Hi, Annabelle," I say. "Sunny and I can help decorate your side of the room—or maybe we can conjure up some wall hangings in our *special* classes."

Both Sunny and Annabelle love this idea. I have to say, it feels SO good to know *two* witches already.

"So what's in that beautiful chest?" I ask Annabelle.

She grins mischievously.

"Treasure, of course!" she says, and winks. "It's the only special thing I brought from home. I've been collecting what's in that chest for years. Would you like to see?"

Sunny runs over and plunks onto the bed beside Annabelle.

"I can't wait to see the look on Heidi's face when you show her!" Sunny says excitedly to Annabelle. Then she turns to me. "**Prepare to gasp!**"

My eyes widen.

What could possibly be in that trunk?

Annabelle kneels beside her antique chest and unlatches the clasp on the front. Then she slowly opens the lid.

Of course I *do* gasp and cover my mouth with my hand when I see what's inside. The chest is filled to the brim with sparkling crystals and dazzling gemstones.

It's the most beautiful sight I've ever seen.

It's nothing like Henry's pirate treasure, which is just a bunch of pathetic plastic gold coins and shiny strands of Mardi Gras beads.

"Annabelle, your gems are stunning!"

All I want to do is dip both hands into the trunk and feel them against my skin.

"Go ahead," Annabelle says as if she has read my mind. "Plunge your hands into the chest!"

I kneel in front of the chest and slide both hands into the polished gems and nubbly crystals. Then I scoop them up and let them fall gently from my hands, examining each stone's beauty.

"I've never seen *anything* like this! What do you use them for, Annabelle?" And I instantly regret saying this, because obviously they're for charms and spells.

I feel like such a dork.

But Annabelle welcomes my question.

"My gift as a witch is healing and wellness," she says in that gorgeous accent. "I love to find cures for people and animals who are sick, injured, or sad. It's always been my special strength. What about you, Heidi? What's your strength as a witch?"

Immediately my thoughts plummet.

Oh no! Not THIS again! I, of course, have no idea about my so-called special gift!

All I collect are trinkets from gumball machines and fast-food kid's meals, and Annabelle heals people with gems and crystals, while Sunny harnesses the power of the sun to work magic.

Suddenly I feel like a giant—*no, make that* **ENORMOUS, all caps**—LOSER.

I sigh heavily. Again, I panic.

What if I don't have a special gift?

What if I'm just some average, run-of-the-mill witch who can only move things with her mind once in a while?

"I wish I *knew*," I say pathetically.

Annabelle laughs it off, like no big deal. "Don't worry, Heidi. You'll figure out what your gift is soon enough, and when you do, it'll be so natural, like you've known all along."

Sunny nods because **she said the exact same thing.**

"I hope you are right," I say, gazing back into the chest of gems and crystals. "**I wonder what my gift will be?**"

Sunny pats my shoulder. "It'll be something amazing, Heidi, just like you. You have to promise to tell us when you figure it out."

I stand up. "You will be the first to know!"

Then I look at the time on my phone. "I have to head back to Baileywick. My RA is picking me up for dinner in ten minutes."

Sunny bounces off the bed. "We're going to the cafeteria at six. See you there, Heidi!"

I head for the door.

"Nice to meet you!" Annabelle adds.

"Same. See you both in a bit!"

I hurry along the hall and down the floating stairs.

I'm feeling haunted by my tragic lack of a special gift.

Merg.

I hope I figure this out soon.

And more important, I hope I actually *have* a special gift!

I step outside into the rain and dash to my dorm. My bun unravels as I run. I slide my scrunchie around my wrist.

When I get to my door, I stop to catch my breath.

I hear rustling sounds inside the room.

That must mean my roommate's back!

Oh yay!

I can't wait to meet her!

I really hope we get along. Before I enter, I quickly remind myself:

Don't be quick to judge!

Give her a chance!

Then I twist the knob—*Eee!*—and open the door . . .

DOOMMATES

. . . and that's when I get the *shock* of my life—an absolute, nearly faint, knees-turn-to-jelly shock!

My broommate is *Melanie Maplethorpe!*

I open my mouth and scream. Melanie jumps back, and her blue eyes seem to pop out of her face, like on a rubber squeeze toy.

What's going on?! I cry to myself as I stand face-to-face with . . .

Melanie,

my Number One Enemy . . .

and my Number Two Reason for Leaving Brewster.

All I've ever wanted was to get away from this girl! Is this some kind of cruel joke? Or did I fall through an invisible portal? Maybe that weird old elevator transported me to the Land of Absolutely No Way!

Melanie jolts me out of my thoughts.

"Heidi Heckelbeck?! What are YOU doing here?"

She sounds not only shocked but scared, which is exactly how I feel.

"This is *my* room!" I say defiantly. "The question is, what are YOU doing here?" Then I let go of the doorknob and put my hand to my forehead. Am I sick or something? Am I having a nightmare?

Somebody please tell me this is a dream or a frightening mirage or anything but REAL.

Melanie folds her arms against her chest. She always does this when she wants to gain control of a situation. Then she glares at me with her slightly upturned nose and that almighty, *I'm-better-than-you* look on her face.

"Okay, Heidi, this is as much of a shock to me as it is to *you. Obviously.* The last thing I ever dreamed was that you would go to Broomsfield and that we would wind up being *broommates.* And if I did dream of it, it was **definitely a nightmare.**"

I stare at Melanie, dumbfounded.

Why is this happening?

It feels like I've been on an emotional roller coaster all day!

First I leave the comfort of my home and town, then I find out I don't have a special gift as a witch, and now I learn that my broommate—*or should I say "doommate"*—is the only person I've never liked.

How are we supposed to LIVE together?

Am I completely cursed?

My eyes begin to burn and I feel like I'm going to cry, but I can't because I wouldn't want to give Melanie the pleasure of watching me have a meltdown. I just don't understand why Melanie has always been so mean to me. **What did I ever do to her?** She seems to have hated me from the instant she laid eyes on me.

I have no words. But Melanie has all kinds of words, **and none of them are nice.**

"No offense, *Heidi,* but there is NO WAY we can be broommates," she says, like this is something *she* has control over. "Fortunately," she goes on, "I know people in *high* places, and they'll move me to a better dorm. I'll even request a room all to myself."

Now I fold *my* arms because, of course, only privileged Melanie knows the *right* people to contact in every situation. She sure seems confident that somehow she's just solved our problem, and nothing would make me happier if those *people in high places* could fix such a glaringly incorrect broommate match, but I seriously doubt the school will make an exception— even for Melanie. Broomsfield is all about students learning to get along with all kinds of people, though Melanie and I might be an exception to *that* theory.

And I honestly think she *should* have a room to herself.

Nobody should have to be subjected to living with Melanie Maplethorpe.

But I keep these thoughts to myself as Melanie blabbers on. She has fallen right back into her comfortable routine of making rude remarks about me to my face. She's done this since second grade. You'd think I could handle it by now, but I can't. It still hurts, and somehow I'm always caught in the crosshairs of her ugly rants, like right now.

"So, Heidi," she says, sounding snootier than ever, "how did you get your hair to stick to your face like that?"

I wipe my wet hair out of my face. Hasn't Melanie ever heard of RAIN? Or humidity? Probably not because somehow *Melanie's* hair always looks perfect no matter what the weather is doing. And honestly, I don't know why Melanie loves to insult me. It seems like her favorite pastime. If you don't *dress* like Melanie, *act* like Melanie, or *worship* Melanie, she'll put you down. But I have to admit, she's right about my hair. I *do* need to fix it, but she doesn't have to make me feel bad. I'm so mad, I make her letter *M* light box go magically askew. Then I stomp into the bathroom without responding to her rude comment.

I look at myself in the bathroom mirror.

My hair DID frizz out in the rain. *Eek!* It's time to perform some hair magic. I don't want Melanie to get suspicious, so I turn on my hair dryer and wave it around to make it sound like I'm styling my hair. It also gives me time to try to grasp the idea of having **Melanie, the Princess of Pink, as my broommate.** I think I'd rather live with a pink flamingo or maybe a pink elephant. There has to be a way out of this roommate situation. Fingers crossed that she'll get a room transfer, but if worse comes to worst, this might be a situation where it would be worth breaking the rules just a tiny bit and using a little magic outside class. And that reminds me, I'll have to *hide* the fact that I'm a witch from her.

Ugh, I can't even relax in my own room.

Merg!

Somebody knocks on the door to our room. It must be Jenna picking us up for dinner. I switch off the hair dryer and magically fix my hair. *Voila!* It's clean, dry, shiny, and gorgeous. I step back into the room. Jenna smiles at me with her ultra-cheery grin.

"Hey, Heidi! I was just telling Melanie how awesome your room looks! You both have great style." Normally I don't mind compliments and cheeriness, but I'm not up for it right now, so I force a smile. Then we follow Jenna into the hall. As the door shuts, I use a little magic to make Melanie's letter *M* light box fall all the way onto the floor. That makes me feel a teensy bit better.

Jenna talks all the way to the cafeteria. Melanie and I don't say a word. I'm sure Jenna must wonder why we're so quiet.

Our table assignments are listed on the bulletin board in the cafeteria. Jenna says we change tables until we have a chance to meet everyone.

And guess who's at my table?

Smell-a-nie Maple-Thorn-in-My-Shoe, of course.

Ugh.

I spy Sunny at the table across from mine. Annabelle is sitting next to her. I wish I could tell Sunny what's gone down since I left her room. **She'd never believe it.**

Dinner is chicken (or barbecued tofu for the vegetarian option), rice, broccoli, and corn. I basically have zero appetite, so I push the food around on my plate to make it look like I'm eating. Nobody even notices. The other kids at the table, except Melanie, are all gabbing away with Jenna. I half listen to the conversation about orientation, which starts tomorrow.

Then I notice Sunny waving at me. She has a silly grin on her face. *What is that girl up to?* I wonder. Sunny picks up a piece of broccoli from her plate and holds it up to her ear. Then she does the same on the other side of her head. It looks like she has two broccoli flowers coming out of her ears!

I burst out laughing.

Everybody at my table stops talking and looks at me.

I shrug and look away. They must think it's a little weird that I went from a scowling face to explosive laughter. I watch Sunny put down the broccoli. She points to the drink station. I'm pretty sure she wants to meet me there. I quickly excuse myself and make a beeline for the drink station.

"Sunny, you are SO hilarious!" I say. Sunny laughs and rolls her eyes, like it's normal to pretend to stick cooked vegetables into your ears.

BRAINSSSS

Lol!

"Well, I had to do SOMETHING. You looked like a zombie over there. Is something wrong?"

I take a deep breath and nod. "MORE than wrong. The *unthinkable* has happened."

Sunny's brow wrinkles with confusion. "What are you talking about?"

I look over at Melanie and then back at Sunny. "It turns out my broommate is a girl from my hometown—somebody I've never gotten along with, ever. We're total opposites and she's super-mean and stuck-up, and somehow we are now living in the same room. I'm totally freaking out right now."

Sunny glances at my table and picks out Melanie in

a heartbeat. "Is she the one with the pink ponytail holder and fashion-Barbie clothes?"

I nod. "BINGO."

Sunny shakes her head. "I'm really sorry, Heidi, but please try not to worry. These things have a way of working out. Maybe you two will learn to get along. It's not like you're in elementary school anymore. Plus you don't have to hang out with her all the time. You can always hang out with Annabelle and me instead!"

Sunny lays her arm around my shoulder. She's such a caring person, but I still can't imagine being friends with Melanie. We've had very brief moments of getting along in the past, but we *always* go back to our old roles of despising each other.

"Thanks for understanding, Sunny. I doubt Melanie and I will ever get along. She hasn't liked me since the day we met."

Sunny frowns. "How could anyone *not* like

you, Heidi? You're the best! We can talk about it more tomorrow. Hang in there!"

Thank goodness for Sunny, I think. *I would be lost here without her!*

I nod appreciatively, and we head back to our tables.

Later, when we get back to the dorm, Jenna introduces everyone on our floor to our housemother, Mrs. Kettledrum. She's in charge of Baileywick, and she's also a teacher at the school. She has strawberry-blond hair, like mine. Jenna says Mrs. Kettledrum has been at Broomsfield since, like, forever. *Whoa.* And before that she was a student, like us. She must really *love* this place! That must be a good sign. I wonder if she knew my mom and Aunt Trudy when they went here. Maybe I'll get the chance to ask her someday.

Everyone on our floor gathers in Mrs. Kettledrum's apartment. She stands in the middle of the room

and holds a large empty basket in her hands, and
nobody is prepared for what happens next.

"What I'm going to ask of each one of you isn't
going to be easy," Mrs. Kettledrum begins. "But
trust me, you'll all get used to it, and before long
you'll even appreciate it." Everybody looks around
the room at each other like, *Uh-oh, what's
she talking about?* We don't have to
wonder for long.

"I want everyone to place their cell phone in this basket." A group moan circles around the room.

"Now, here's how it'll work," she continues. "I'll keep your phones during the week, and on Friday after last period, you may have your phones until Sunday night."

Her words are met with more moans and groans. I'm not thrilled with the news either, but my parents have strict cell phone rules, so it's not that big a deal. But Melanie is not taking the cell phone news well at all.

The color completely drains from her face.

I think she may be in shock.

The phone is probably her only real friend, or maybe she's never been told she can't have something.

One by one we drop our phones into the basket. When Mrs. Kettledrum gets to Melanie,

Melanie doesn't put her phone in the basket. Instead she whispers something to Mrs. Kettledrum. We can all hear it.

"Um, my parents have given me special privileges to keep my phone at school. It's for emotional support reasons." A couple of girls snicker. Mrs. Kettledrum smiles knowingly.

"Melanie, dear, do you think I haven't heard that one before?" she says, holding the basket closer to Melanie. "You can part with your phone for a few days. I promise, you *will* survive."

Melanie holds her phone close. She must feel the pressure of us all watching. She finally musters the courage to hold her phone over the basket, but she still doesn't let go of it.

"The faster you let it go, Melanie, the sooner we can move on to our surprise," Mrs. Kettledrum says.

Some of the girls are getting mad.

"Just drop it!" one girl says. "Do you think you're more special than the rest of us?" At this point Melanie can't take the pressure anymore and drops her phone into the basket. She yelps and hides her face. It's weirdly entertaining.

"Well done, Melanie!" Mrs. Kettledrum says. "And now for the *good* news!" We stand, cell-phone-less, and wait for it.

"Tonight we're going to watch a movie in my apartment, followed by homemade cookies and milk. The movie is *Freaky Friday*, and showtime is *now*."

I love *Freaky Friday*. It's one of my favorite movies, and it makes me wonder: *Would a spell like the one in the movie work on Melanie and me? What if Melanie and I switched bodies? Would it make us see each other differently? Maybe, but with my luck we would get stuck in each other's bodies FOREVER.*

And *that* is a truly terrifying thought.

Mrs. Kettledrum clicks the movie icon on her computer as everybody finds a place to sit—everybody, that is, except me. I have another plan.

"Heidi, please turn out the lights," Mrs. Kettledrum says, pointing to a switch beside the door. I dash over and flick the switch. Then I hurry back to Mrs. Kettledrum.

"May I come back *after* the movie for the cookie party?" I ask. "I need to finish unpacking." I know I'm bending the truth, since I'm already unpacked, but I *really* need some alone time.

And good news! Mrs. Kettledrum actually says yes.
What a relief!

When I get back to my room, it's quiet and peaceful.
I flick on my twinkly lights and my new desk lamp.
Then I sit at my desk for the first time. It feels
good, though still a little strange and unfamiliar.

I open my desk drawer and pull out my new
stationery from Aunt Trudy and a purple pen. The

cards are so pretty. Each one has a different-color border: hot pink, pistachio green, orange, purple, and aqua. My name is written across the top in pink raised letters: HEIDI HELENA HECKELBECK. The envelope liners have matching stripes. Aunt Trudy gave me a hundred cards so I could write to my friends and family whenever I want to, but my aunt is the only person I want to write to right now, so here goes!

*H*EIDI *H*ELENA *H*ECKELBECK

Dear Aunt Trudy,

I've only been at Broomsfield for a few hours, and SO much has happened already. Some of my news is good, and some of it's terrible. Here's the good stuff: You're never going to believe this, but I'm in Baileywick—**your old dorm!** I'm in Room 307.

Can you believe it?

That made me so happy.

Then, this afternoon, I bumped into my friend Sunny Akhtar. Remember her from our beach trip years ago? She's really awesome, and I'm so happy to have a friend, and not only that but she's also a witch. **Woo!** So that's the end of the good news.

Now for the bad stuff. I found out from Sunny that she has a special gift as a witch. She can use the power of the sun to perform spells. Isn't that cool? Then I found out her roommate, Annabelle, has a special gift too. She can heal people and animals with gems and crystals. Now, you may wonder why this is bad news. Well, it made me realize that I don't HAVE a special gift as a witch. Why didn't you or Mom ever talk to me about this? Am I just a boring, ordinary witch with nothing special about me? Do you think this will change? My friends said I would probably figure out my special gift at boarding school. But I'm not sure. I haven't had so much as a whiff of something special. I would love to know your thoughts on this, Aunt Trudy. Also, have you ever noticed anything special about my witch skills? Please don't hold back!

Okay, now it's time for the really bad news. You'd better sit down because, I'm not kidding, it's whopping bad news. Are you sitting yet? I really don't want you to fall over when you hear it. I'm still reeling. Ready?

My roommate is MELANIE MAPLETHORPE. **This is not a joke.** I got stuck with Melanie, my only enemy on planet Earth. I know you must be almost as shocked as I am. What am I going to do? There are SO many reasons why I don't like

Melanie. Here's a short list:

She's mean.
She thinks she's better than me.
She insults me and puts me down all the time.
She's faker than all the animals in the stuffed animal section of a toy store.
She's obsessed with her looks.
She brags nonstop.
She's totally stuck-up.
She makes me feel bad about myself.

HEIDI HELENA HECKELBECK

Believe me, I can think of many more reasons why I don't like Melanie, but you get the idea.

Why is this happening to me, Aunt Trudy?

One of the things I was looking forward to at Broomsfield was never having to see Melanie again. But instead we wind up not only at the same school but in the same ROOM. I'm stuck with the Girl of DOOM!

What should I do???????

Wish I had better news.
I miss you and love you SO much.

♥ ♥ ♥ ♥ ♥ ♥ ♥

Heidi

P.S. Give your cats a pet from me!

I tuck the letter inside an envelope, address it, stamp it, and seal it with a heart sticker. Now to mail it, but the only problem is, the mail room isn't open and I really need her to get this letter ASAP.

Then I have an idea. . . .

Mom says only to use magic in an emergency, I think. Well, this is sort of an emergency. I'm really down, and the only thing that's going to make me feel better is hearing from Aunt Trudy, fast.

I quickly gather the ingredients and cast an overnight-mail spell.

Whoosh! My letter disappears.

I feel a little bit guilty for using a spell outside class, but I quickly override this feeling.

This is a real emergency, so it is a good use of magic, I tell myself. Aunt Trudy needs to get my letter as *soon* as possible.

The movie is probably over by now, so I race back down the hall to Mrs. Kettledrum's apartment. Everyone's already having homemade chocolate chip cookies and milk when I get there. That's when I realize, *I'm starving.* I haven't eaten a thing all day on my emotional roller coaster! I down two cookies and a tall glass of milk. *Ahhhhh.* I feel better already. Then I meet a few other girls on my hall. They all seem really nice. As for Melanie and me, we're still totally ignoring each other. **I'm dreading going back to the room with her.**

And I have a funny feeling that it's going to be a very *looooong* night.

GAME ON!

Melanie stands in front of the full-length mirror in our room for a long time.

Does she think this is her own *personal full-length mirror?* I wonder.

She already has on her pj's—a light gray tank top with pink-and-gray-plaid shorts.

She brushes her long blond hair and completely ignores me.

Whatever.

I grab my pajamas and change in the bathroom.

When I come out, Melanie's in bed with her eyes shut. She has on a pair of pink plush over-the-ear headphones.

I hop onto my bed with the scrapbook Lucy gave me and pore over the pages. I love seeing pictures of my friends and me, but it makes me sad, too.

Lucy wrote funny captions underneath each picture like, AN APPLE A DAY HELPS KEEP DOROTHY AWAY.

I laugh out loud because it's a picture of our second-grade play, *The Wizard of Oz,* and Melanie played Dorothy, and I played one of those ridiculous talking apple trees.

The only upside was, I got to throw apples at Dorothy, aka Melanie.

Lol!

I glance across the room to see if Melanie woke up when I laughed. Nope, her eyes are still shut. I want to make sure she's *really* asleep, so I do a little test.

"Melanie?" I say in my daytime voice. Melanie doesn't move. She's definitely asleep.

Perfect.

Now I can hide *my* Book of Spells *and medallion.*

I cannot leave them anywhere Melanie might see them and have her figure out that I'm a witch.

That's my own *private* business.

I close my scrapbook and slide off my bed. Then I wrap my *Book of Spells* and medallion in one of my towels and tuck it back into my mini suitcase. I push the suitcase way under my bed.

Melanie had better not snoop.

I crawl under the covers and switch off my light.

Ahhhhh, it feels so good to relax after the longest day of my life. But then I realize . . .

I CAN'T relax!

I can hear something that sounds worse than an army of flies.

I sit up in bed.

What's that NOISE?

It doesn't make me long to realize what it is.

It's music leaking from Melanie's headphones,
only it doesn't sound like music. It sounds like an
electronic chipmunk band.

UGH! How am I going to get to sleep NOW?!

Then *ping!* An idea pops into my head.

I know! I'll just magically remove Melanie's pesky
headphones.

She'll never know. So I focus my magical
attention on her headphones.

One, two, three. Whoosh!

The headphones fly right off her head.

Then I magically swoosh them into the bathroom
and shut the door. Melanie doesn't stir at all, but
in the moonlight I can see I've made her hair stick
straight up in front, like a unicorn horn.

Oops.

I lie back down and let out a long, satisfying sigh, and *poof!* I fall sound asleep.

✧ ✧ ✧

In the morning a tidal wave of apple blossoms, lilies of the valley, and mandarin oranges washes over me. I sit up and pinch my nose.

"*EW!* What's that SMELL?"

Melanie is on her way to the bathroom, but I spy an uncapped perfume bottle sitting on her dresser. It's called Runway Girl.

Seriously? It should *be called Run for Your Life, Girl!*

Guess I won't need an alarm clock this year. I have my own private stink bomb instead.

"Hey!" Melanie shouts from the bathroom. "How'd my headphones get into the SINK? Wait . . . why is my hair sticking up in the front?"

I try not to laugh as I hop out of bed.

"Maybe you put them there in your sleep," I suggest. Melanie doesn't respond.

I can hear her jump into the shower, probably to shampoo her hair back down, so I go to my dresser and pick out my clothes for orientation.

Jenna told us to wear something comfy. I pull on my light gray capri leggings and a sage-green tank top. I finish the outfit with my white jean jacket and green-striped sneakers.

Melanie walks out of the bathroom, looks me up and down, and shakes her head.

Whatever, I think.

She has on a short white skirt, a pink top, a gray cardigan, and white sneakers. *Her* style isn't *my* style, but that doesn't mean I hate what she's wearing.

Why does she always have to put down *my* style?

I shake it off and dash into the bathroom. I give myself a magic mani and make my nails sage green to match my top. I feel a little guilty using magic, but not really.

What kind of witch does her nails by hand? It's too time-consuming and impossible to stay in the lines. *As if!*

Clump!

The door to our room clunks shut. **Melanie must've left for breakfast without me.**

SO rude!

But to be fair, I would've done the same if I had been ready first.

I shake off the bad Melanie vibes and put on my sparkly moon-and-star earrings.

I got my ears pierced over the summer. *Woo!*

I grab my backpack and shove my orientation folder inside. Then I walk to the cafeteria by myself, and that "new girl" feeling sweeps over me again.

Hello, Earthlings! I say to myself in alien talk. *I'm. From. The. Planet. Brewster. I. Come. In. Peace . . . !*

I scan the room. Everyone looks cheerful and happy, talking away. I wonder when the "new girl" feeling will end and I'll feel like part of this school.

What if it never ends?

Chatter fills the cafeteria, along with the clink of utensils and the clank of plates. I take a seat at our table. Jenna passes around a serving bowl of oatmeal and another bowl with scrambled eggs. I let both pass by.

I get up to explore the other breakfast options. The breakfast station has toast, bagels, English muffins, cereal, yogurt, and fruit. I grab some cereal and a banana.

I'm so happy they have cereal—that's one worry crossed off my list.

After breakfast we have an assembly in the auditorium. Principal Ray talks about the rules and expectations for the year.

Then we meet in groups for orientation. I'm in Group Five.

We gather outside the Barn on the lawn. The RAs

hold up signs with our group numbers. Jenna has Group Five.

Yay, I like her—she's really nice. I jog over, and I'm the first one there. I say hi to Jenna and wait for the others.

Please don't let Melanie be in my group, I think, crossing my fingers.

Then I see Sunny and Annabelle coming.

"Are you two in Group Five?"

They both nod, and all three of us squeal for joy.

And to make things even *more* interesting, the boy with the honey-colored bangs and green eyes who said hi to me on the path yesterday is *also* in our group.

Woo!

He's so ridiculously cute, I have to look the other way.

Well, I don't want him to think I *like* him! *Eeesh!*

"Welcome, Hunter McCann!" Jenna says, and checks him off her list.

Okay, now I know Cute Guy's REAL name, so from now on I officially dub him McCutie.

Another girl shows up with long dark hair, skin with not a pimple in sight, braces, and high cheekbones. She's in a wheelchair, and one of her legs is in a cast. Her name is Viviane DeCastro. She pronounces her name Vivi-*ahni,* but she goes by Vivi.

Then a tall boy with curly dark hair and blue eyes joins the group. He sidles up next to Hunter McCutie. Jenna takes a head count.

"Everyone's here! Let's make some quick intros, and then I'll tell you what we're doing this morning. I guarantee you're going to love it!" Jenna has us introduce ourselves and say where we're from and something about ourselves.

Hunter—*aka Mr. McCutie*—is from California, and he loves baseball and reading. The pretty girl with

the long dark hair, Vivi, is from Brazil, and she's
into gymnastics and soccer. She tells us she broke
her leg tumbling and has to be in a wheelchair
to keep the weight off her leg. The boy with the
dark curls is Tate Harris. He's from New Jersey,
and he likes soccer, music, and video games. Then
there's Sunny, Annabelle, and me.

The best thing about our group is that there's absolutely *no* Melanie.

Melanie is in Group Four, which is right next to
us. I try my best not to look at her, but my eyes
are weirdly drawn to her. Maybe because she
makes me so uneasy. Melanie catches me looking
and wrinkles her pert little nose. Ugh! I quickly
look away.

Jenna tells us we're going on a scavenger hunt to
get to know our way around campus and also to
get to know one another.

As Jenna leads our group to the starting place,
Sunny leans in close.

"I have something to tell you," she whispers. "I think there are more witches sitting at my table in the cafeteria."

"How can you tell?" I ask.

"It happened at dinner yesterday," Sunny says. "I didn't think much of it then, but one girl took a bite of her food and said, 'STT.' Then two other kids nodded like they agreed with her. Then at breakfast this morning it happened again! A boy looked at his plate and said, 'STT!'"

"So?" I say. I am completely baffled.

"So?" Sunny replies. "It must be some sort of a code! Or part of a spell! A witch's spell! Don't worry. I'll get to the bottom of it."

I am not sure, but Sunny seems excited. I just nod my head in agreement.

"Okay, so the scavenger hunt is also a *race*," Jenna begins, once we get to the starting point. "Whichever group collects all their stickers first wins a special prize. And remember, everybody in the group has to get a sticker on their card at each station—not just one of you—*all of you*."

As soon as our group knows it's a race, we look at one another like, *Let's win this thing.*

Vivi and Tate give each other a high five, and Annabelle and Sunny shout, "Go, Group Five!" I glance at Melanie again.

What is my problem?

It's like Melanie is some bizarre Heidi magnet.

Or maybe I just need to know where my enemy is at all times.

Melanie catches me—*again*—and narrows her eyes.

Then she points both of her thumbs *down*.

Wait, is Melanie challenging me?

Does she think her team can beat *our* team?

Suddenly my competitive side kicks into gear.

I feel fierce.

GAME ON, I think.

Now our team HAS to beat Melanie's *no matter what.*

"Yeah, Group Five is gonna win!" I yell, maybe a little too loudly, but I smile when the rest of my group—including Hunter—all shouts in agreement.

Jenna passes out our clues and a campus map, and explains the rules.

"You have to work as a *team.*

"Nobody is allowed to separate from the group to find clues faster.

"This is about getting to know the people in your group as well as getting to know the campus.

"*Got it?*

"Collect your stickers, and place them beside each clue.

"Principal Ray will start the race when all the groups are ready.

"We'll meet back here when you've gotten all your stickers."

I turn to my team and clap my hands.

"Huddle!" I say. Our team gathers around. I am so ready to do this!

"Okay, we *have* to win. For me it's personal."

Sunny knows what I'm talking about and looks over at Melanie's group and then back at me.

"Be careful, Heidi," she warns. "Make sure your motives for winning are *good*."

Annabelle says the same thing.

The boys roll their eyes. I do too.

Why should I worry about my motives? I wonder.

I only have ONE motive—to beat Melanie!

What's so bad about THAT?

"Teams, take your marks!" Principal Ray calls. All the teams stop talking and focus on the principal, except me. I'm reading the first clue.

Principal Ray raises an air horn over her head. "Ready! Set! Go!" She blows the horn.

Some of the groups take off running. I lean into our group and read the first clue out loud.

"Fuzzy Wuzzy was a WHAT?"

"A BEAR!" we all cry. Everyone knows that the bear is our school's mascot.

We're the Broomsfield Bears!

"So where would we find the mascot?" I ask, because I seriously have *no* idea where the mascot lives, but the boys seem to know.

"Mascots show up at sporting events," Hunter says softly so other teams won't hear. "Let's check out the playing field with the bleachers."

We find the playing field on the map and take off running. Vivi whizzes ahead of us.

"Go, Bears!" she cries.

At the field we spy the mascot handing out stickers to another group.

Oh no! It's Melanie's group!

Once Melanie's team leaves on their way to discover the next clue, the mascot comes over to our group. **We get stickers and high fives.**

"Go, Bears!" Vivi says one more time before we say goodbye to the mascot.

Annabelle reads the next clue. "What building has the most *stories*?"

Everybody's thinking of the tallest buildings, but I've heard this one before. **"The *LIBRARY* has the most *stories*—get it?!"**

We zoom back onto the path and chase Vivi to the library, which is super-modern, like Sunny's dorm.

We stampede through the entrance. **This library is SO cool.**

It has all kinds of cozy places to curl up with a book.

There are carpeted reading nooks built *into the walls.* Each one is round and has a mini reading light and fuzzy pillows too. There are even sunken couches in the floor, and study tables weave around the library like a maze.

Wow, studying might actually be FUN in here.

We race to the circulation desk, and the librarian is waiting for scavenger hunters. She instantly looks familiar. I know I've met her before.

Wait! I think. *This is the SAME librarian from the magical library in Brewster!*

"Hi, Ms. Egli!" I say. "Remember me? I thought you worked in Brewster!"

She laughs and winks at me.

"Of course I remember you, Heidi! **Welcome to Broomsfield!**"

She places a sticker on my card. "And I *do* work in Brewster, but only part-time. This is my full-time gig."

Then she hands out stickers to the rest of our team.

Seeing Ms. Egli makes me feel more connected to Broomsfield—just like running into

Sunny made me feel yesterday—but there's no time to think or linger.

Time to race on!

"Gotta go!" I say as our team runs toward the door. Meanwhile, I've lost track of Melanie's team.

What if she's ahead of us?

I can't let *that* happen.

I read the next clue while we're running.

"Find the old dairy farm!" I say.

Then I lower my voice so only our group will hear. "It's the Barn!" I tell them. Then I sprint down the path.

"Wait up!" Annabelle cries. I look over my shoulder.

"Hurry!" I shout, because there's no stopping me now.

We *have* to win.

Luckily, Sunny slows down and waits for
Annabelle.

"Meet you there!" I yell over my shoulder. The boys
catch up to me. Vivi pulls ahead in her chair.

Melanie's team isn't at the Barn either.

Maybe that's a good sign, I tell myself.

OR maybe it's NOT.

Better keep moving.

We collect our stickers and work on the
next two clues while we wait for Sunny and
Annabelle.

"Who has the most patients at Broomsfield?"
Vivi asks. "And it's spelled like patients that need
a doctor."

Tate's face lights up. "The infirmary!"

I read the next clue without even thanking Tate for getting the last one. "Too much homework makes some students climb the walls."

The boys get this one too. "The rock-climbing gym," Hunter says.

"Good one," I say, and I'm about to read the next clue when Sunny and Annabelle walk in. I look up from my clues.

"Hurry up and grab your stickers!" I shout. "We already have the next two clues figured out."

Sunny and Annabelle roll their eyes as they go get their stickers.

What's their *problem?* I wonder.

I'm helping us *win* this scavenger hunt!

Sheesh.

I read the next clue.

"People are *drawn* to this room."

"I know the answer," Vivi says. "It's the art room because people are *drawn* to it. Get it?"

I quickly write down Vivi's answer as well as the answers to the last two clues so we don't forget.

"One more clue before we head out," I say. "This one's from Shakespeare. 'All the world's a stage, and all the men and women merely players.'"

I answer—*once again*—before anyone else has a chance. "The auditorium!

"Let's go!"

The rest of my team looks at each other and then back at me as if I've lost my mind or something.

"What?" I say. "I just want to beat *Mel*—I mean, I just want to *win* this thing!"

Annabelle shakes her head. "Wow, Heidi, you're *so* competitive! Is that an American thing?"

I take off and answer on the run.

"Nope, it's a ME thing!"

And my team has no choice but to follow me. We stop at the infirmary, the gym, and the art room. We're racking up stickers. I can tell my team is a little tired of me pushing them so hard.

But too bad!

That's what it takes to win.

I charge toward the auditorium and applaud myself on the way for not using magic.

Way to go, Heidi!

No sooner have I thought this than I roll my ankle *really hard.*

"Ooooow!" I scream, and crumple to the ground. My team stops and gathers around me.

"Heidi, are you OKAY?" Sunny asks.

I shake my head as I rock back and forth.

"Noooooo," I cry. I can't stop moaning.

This is TERRIBLE!

What if I can't complete the scavenger hunt?

What if Melanie's team wins!

This can't be happening!

Sunny and Annabelle kneel beside me. Sunny tells Vivi and the boys to keep going and we'll meet them at the auditorium. Then she turns back to me.

"Can you move your foot at all?" Sunny asks. I shake my head.

Annabelle gently inspects my ankle. It's
swelling.

"I wish I'd brought some of my healing crystals, but I
didn't want to get caught using magic."

I lean back on both hands and look at my friends.

"I am SO sorry. I've ruined the scavenger
hunt, and now we're going to lose!"

Sunny folds her arms. "Heidi, you haven't ruined anything," she says. "You just pushed things a little too far."

I know Sunny's right, and then I remember what she said earlier about having good motives about the scavenger hunt.

Maybe my motives *were* a little out of whack.

"This is all because I wanted to beat Melanie.

"If her team wins, I'll never hear the end of it."

Sunny sits down beside me.

"Well, how would you like to finish the scavenger hunt for the *right* reasons?" she asks. "If you do, then maybe I can help you, but first you need to have a change of heart."

I hear what Sunny is saying, but I'm having a wrestling match in my head.

One side of my brain knows Sunny's right.

The other side of my brain says I don't want to lose to Melanie.

Why is this SO hard?

I sit forward, and my ankle moves a little bit. I wince with pain.

OW!

I lean back and shut my eyes and wait for the pain to die down. Then I think about what Jenna said at the start of the scavenger hunt.

It was supposed to be about making friends and getting to know the campus, and I turned it into a personal battle with Melanie.

Now I've let down my teammates, including Hunter McCutie, who probably thinks I'm totally obnoxious and will never like me now.

Ugh!

What is wrong with me?

The last thing I want is to alienate everybody.

So what DO you want? I ask myself.

Suddenly an answer comes to me.

"I think I have a better motive," I say, still holding my ankle.

"All I really want is for everyone to have a good time."

Sunny and Annabelle look at each other and smile.

"I can work with that!" Sunny says. Then she looks toward the sun and begins to chant.

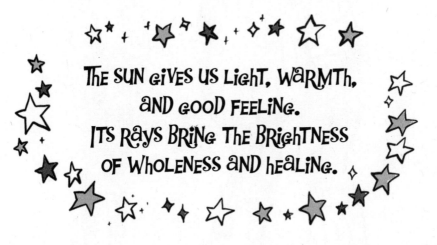

THE SUN GIVES US LIGHT, WARMTH,
AND GOOD FEELING.
ITS RAYS BRING THE BRIGHTNESS
OF WHOLENESS AND HEALING.

Immediately I feel the pain drain from my ankle. I twirl my foot in a circular motion. It feels normal and strong. I hop up and test it.

It WORKS!

And now I know what it means *to jump for joy*!

"Sunny, my ankle is all better! You're amazing."

Sunny stands up. "You did most of the work, Heidi. It all had to do with what you were thinking."

I hug Sunny. Not only does my ankle feel better but I also feel calm, **and the pressure to win is gone.**

Don't get me wrong. I still want to win, but not because I want to get back at somebody else.

"Well, what are we waiting for?" Annabelle says. "Let's go!"

I run over to Annabelle. "Wait, first I want to give you something." I hold out my arms and give Annabelle a hug.

"I'm sorry I didn't wait for you," I say.

Annabelle hugs me back. "Never mind. It's all forgotten."

The rest of the scavenger hunt is a ton of fun. We collect all our stickers and report back to the Barn.

There's a picnic waiting for everyone.

We munch on sandwiches and chips as the winners are announced.

And did our team win?

Nope.

But Melanie's team didn't win either. Her team got disqualified because some of the players forgot to get stickers.

Our team took second place, and we got coupons for FREE milkshakes at the snack bar.

But the best part of the whole morning was being with my new friends, getting to know the campus, and secretly crushing on Hunter McCann.

I like Broomsfield so much better today, even though I still WISH, with all my heart, that Melanie wasn't here.

I'm not gonna lie.

I still have a touch of the Melanie mergs.

6

NiGHT TERRORS

I lie in bed and stare at the glow-in-the-dark stars on the ceiling. Whoever lived here before us must have put them up.

And, of course, Melanie has her headphones on again and that tinny chipmunk band is even louder tonight than it was last night. Looks like I'll have to magically remove her headphones again.

I sit up and focus my magic on the headphones, like last night, but this time they won't budge.

What's going on? Did she glue them to her ears?

I try again, but they still stick fast to her head. Why can't I get those silly headphones to move? I flop back onto my pillow.

I'm SO tired, and now Melanie won't even let me sleep! Well, if she won't let me sleep, then I won't let her sleep.

"Melanie, are you AWAKE?"

This time I say it *louder* than my daytime voice—just to be sure. It's best to know if someone's asleep before you perform magic on them, but what if she's *pretending* to be asleep?

Four words: *I'll take my chances.*

I throw off the covers and slide my mini suitcase out from under the bed. I grab my *Book of Spells* and my medallion, and I tiptoe into the bathroom. I find the chapter on pranks.

The last time I used a prank spell was at my fourth-grade slumber party.

I cast the Sand in the Sleeping Bag spell on Laurel Lambert. It didn't go over well, but that gives me an idea.

Maybe I can use the sand from the volleyball court below our window!

All I have to do is magically move it from the sand court into Melanie's bed! That would be a lot easier than casting a spell from my spell book.

I quickly rewrap my *Book of Spells* and medallion in the towel and shove them into the cabinet under the sink for now.

Then I tiptoe back into our room and open the window a crack. I hurry to my bed and dive under the covers.

Then I concentrate really hard.

First I picture the sand in the volleyball court. Then I summon a cup of sand up to the window.

Swoosh!

A stream of sand swirls in through the window. I magically direct the sand in between Melanie's sheets. I squinch my face to hold back the laughter. Then I lie down and pretend to be asleep.

Swish! Swoosh! Swish!

I can hear Melanie's legs swishing under her sheets. She's feeling the grit.

Swoooooosh! Swoooooosh!

Now she's thrashing the sheets with her legs. It's totally working!

Whap! Whap! Thump!

She kicks off the covers and jumps out of bed.

Oh my gosh!

It's so hard not to open my eyes!

But I keep them glued shut. I also breathe rhythmically and heavily as if I'm in a deep sleep.

"Aaaaah!" Melanie shrieks.

I can hear her swiping her sheets with her hands to get the sand out. Sand ticks onto the floor.

"Where did all this SAND come from?!" Melanie cries. She swipes for what seems like forever. Then she switches off her headphones and lays them on her bedside table. The room is quiet.

Mission accomplished! I think.

I hear Melanie crawl back into bed.

"Heidi, I *know* you're behind this!" she says. I don't react, of course. I stay still and keep up the steady breathing. She sighs angrily. "Ugh, you are *so* annoying." Then she rolls over loudly.

The next thing I know, it's midnight! *Oops!* I must've fallen asleep for *real.* Then something tickles my nose.

Achooo!

It tickles again. *ACHOOO!*

It feels like someone is tickling me with a feather.

I wipe my nose with the back of my hand, but it *still* tickles!

Come to think of it, my whole face tickles.

I sit up and rub my face with both hands to get the tickly feeling to stop, and that's when I notice that my arms and legs begin to tickle too.

I frantically rub my body all over to stop the tickling, but it's no use.

It won't stop!

I leap out of bed, run to the bathroom, and turn on the shower.

I dance around the bathroom, waiting for the water to warm up. Then it dawns on me that *Melanie* must be behind this tickle torture.

I'll bet she's getting me back for putting sand in her bed—*so she put feathers in mine!*

I fling my pajamas onto the floor and jump into the shower.

Ahhhhhhhhh. Relief at last!

The water takes away the tickly feeling. But one thing's for sure, this pranking isn't over.

Now it's time for a SERIOUS prank.

I dry off, grab some new pajamas from my dresser, and march back into the bathroom. I unwrap the towel from my *Book of Spells* and go back to the chapter on pranks.

I find the perfect spell.

It's called Night Terrors. A smile blooms on my face as I read the spell:

Night Terrors

Would you like to create a spooky atmosphere for a Halloween party? Or perhaps you'd like to give someone you know the fright of their life? Whatever your scare needs may be, this creepy soundtrack spell will do the trick.

Ingredients

1 set of plastic vampire teeth

3 spooky words

1 fun-size candy bar

5 drops of water

Gather the ingredients together
in a bowl. Hold your Witches
of Westwick medallion in your
left hand and place your right
hand over the mix. Chant the
following spell.

RATTLE! MOAN! WAIL! AND HOWL!
HEAR THE HOOT OF A GREAT HORNED OWL!
CLANKING CHAINS, A CREAKING DOOR.
SOMETHING DRAGS ACROSS THE FLOOR.
GHOSTLY VOICES FILL THE AIR.
CHILLING SOUNDS OF GRIM DESPAIR.
WITH THIS SPELL I WILL SCARE....
AND THOSE WHO HEAR IT BEST BEWARE.

Note: Sounds will last for fifteen minutes.
To add more time, mix in additional
fun-size candy bars. Each bar adds
fifteen minutes of scary sounds.

This is the perfect prank! I think.

And I definitely have ALL the ingredients.

I sneak back into the room and slide my container
of trinkets from under the bed. Then I snag my mini
flashlight, notepad, and pen from my nightstand.
I shine the flashlight on my collection and fish
through for the items I need.

Plastic vampire teeth.

Check.

One fun-size chocolate candy bar.

Check.

Now all I need are three spooky words. I shove the tub back under the bed and take my pad and pen to the bathroom. I glance at Melanie on the way. She's still asleep—unless she's as good at faking as I am. . . .

I place the spell ingredients in the sink. Then I write three spooky words on a piece of paper:

> skeleton
> goblin
> graveyard

I toss the paper in with the other ingredients. Then I gently turn on the faucet and let five drops plink onto the mix. I grab my Witches of Westwick medallion in my left hand, place my right over the mix, and chant the spell.

Poof!

The ingredients vaporize into a mist. *So cool.*
I quickly grab my *Book of Spells* and medallion
and hurry back into the room. The soundtrack has
already started! The first sound is dripping water.

Plip, plop, plip.

The drops echo. *Very creepy.* I shove my
medallion and spell book into the drawer of my
nightstand for now.

Then I crawl under my covers and roll onto my
side with my back to Melanie. The dripping stops.
Now an owl hoots.

Hoo! Hoo! Hoo!

It reminds me of when I went camping with my
family, but it sounds scarier—and much louder—
in our room. The hoots give way to coyotes
howling. Then there's the sound of a door slowly
creaking open. Ghostly voices whisper, but I can't

tell what they're saying. And so far Melanie isn't stirring.

Clump!

A door bangs shut. Even though I know it's the spell, the sudden sound makes *me* flinch. Now it sounds like something is being dragged across the floor.

OMGosh, it's so super-eerie!

If I didn't know it was fake, I'd be terrified. Then I wonder if it is realistic for me to pretend to sleep through all of this. Maybe I should pretend to wake up and act like I don't know what's going on? *Hmmm, not sure.* I should probably pretend to stay asleep.

Now the room is filled with ghostly moaning and wailing sounds, but so far Melanie still hasn't made a peep. She'd better not sleep through this entire spell! What a waste of time THAT would be! But I don't have to worry for long. The cat sound does the trick. The cat begins to growl. The growl grows louder and then erupts into a full-blown catfight.

Hiss! Phttt! Yee-owl!

Screeeeeech!

"Heidi?" Melanie calls out into the dark. "What is happening?" I bite my lip to keep from laughing. I don't dare move or even pretend to wake up. The catfight is over, and a thunderstorm begins to build, with rumbles and cracks in the background.

"Heidi! WAKE UP!" Melanie cries. "Our room is HAUNTED!"

No sooner does she shout this than a stream of maniacal laughter follows. Then I hear feet running.

Wait! THOSE ARE MELANIE'S FEET!

The door to our room opens and slams shut.

Uh-oh, I think.

Where did Melanie GO?

Is she going to TELL on me?!

Oh no! This wasn't supposed to happen!

To make matters worse, I have no way to stop the soundtrack until the fifteen minutes are up.

Oh, HELP!

Now I'm having my *own* night terror!

I lie in bed wishing the spooky soundtrack would end, like, *NOW.*

This isn't funny anymore.

Why was I tempted to use a *real* spell? I could have just walked across the creaking floorboards and made some meowing sounds myself. If I get caught using magic, my parents are going to be furious, and who knows what the school will do? I might even get kicked out before classes begin. I'm SO scared, and it's nobody's fault but my own.

Uh-oh! I hear footsteps coming! The sound is so much scarier than the soundtrack! The doorknob to our room twists. It's all over! Then *BLAMMO!* The soundtrack STOPS before the door opens.

The spell is OVER. I sigh with relief.

I'm SAVED!

Melanie walks back into the room. I can hear Mrs. Kettledrum's voice. My eyes are shut, and I try to keep my breathing as calm as possible so they won't know I'm awake.

"You see, Melanie? Heidi's sound asleep. You probably just had a bad dream. This kind of thing is normal when you leave home for the first time."

I hear Melanie slide back under her covers.

"That's not it!" Melanie says. "Heidi's playing tricks on me, and I *know* it. She's never liked me." Then Melanie's bed creaks. Maybe Mrs. Kettledrum sat on the edge of it.

"I *have* to get a room change," Melanie continues. "Will you *please* talk to someone?"

"We'll see," Mrs. Kettledrum says. "We can talk about it more in the morning. Right now you need to get some rest. Tomorrow's a big day." I hear more shuffling as Mrs. Kettledrum walks toward the door. But then she pauses. I don't dare open my eyes, but I have a suspicion that she has stopped right by my bed. She's probably wondering if I'm actually awake. After a few more moments when I barely breathe, the door to our room opens and then closes. I exhale.

Okay, no more pranks, I tell myself. *Besides, I'm too exhausted anyway.* I fall back to sleep easily.

But not for long. I wake up at three thirty in the morning to the smell of Melanie's overpowering perfume. It's much worse than the tsunami that washed over me yesterday morning. It's more like I'm *swimming* in perfume. I flip over to get away from it, but no matter what direction I

✧ 190 ✧

flip or flop, I can't escape the smell of manufactured flowers and fruit. It's everywhere! **My entire brain smells like Melanie.** I haul myself out of bed—*yet again*—and turn my quilt around so the opposite end is at my head. I take a whiff of my quilt. *Oh, thank goodness! She didn't spray BOTH ends.*

I lie on my pillow with my nose toward the ceiling. It's less stinky this way. I'm way too tired to cast another spell, but I can still *move* stuff. So I do. First I make the window open and close. Then I magically make Melanie's bedding rise and fall. And somewhere in the middle of making Melanie's quilt dance, I fall asleep . . . and stay asleep.

When our alarms go off, neither one of us budges. I hit snooze one, **two, three** times. Finally I sit up in bed. Melanie beat me to the bathroom—yet again. When she comes out, **she glares at me,** and then she and her long blond ponytail sashay out the door.

I'm so relieved. She's gone.

Now I can shower, dress, and feel grumpy all by myself. The shower wakes me up. I get dressed, and today I decide to put on my black-and-white-striped tights. **I instantly feel a million times more like me.** Hopefully I'll feel even better when I see Sunny and Annabelle. Maybe they'll help erase my gloom. Before I leave the room, I check my orientation schedule to see what's going on today. And what's going on is *not* good because today, of course, is . . .

Broommate Bonding Day!

DIS-
ORIENTATION

Broommate Bonding Day means we have to be with our roommates *all* day. Principal Ray says we *must* stick together—no matter what the day brings.

This makes me wonder two things:
1. What *will* the day bring?

And 2. What did I ever do in my years on this planet to deserve this kind of punishment?

I have no answers.

Our first activity is a hike. Jenna hands out a list of let's-get-to-know-you questions that we're supposed to answer on the hike.

This should be fun, I say to myself with the most sarcasm EVER.

What would I like to know about Melanie? I think.

For starters, how about "Why do you hate me?"

How will Melanie and I answer let's-get-to-know-you questions when we're not even talking to each other?

Two words: *We won't.*

We gather for the hike. Melanie and I stand next to each other with our heads turned away. We follow Jenna as she leads us from campus. Sunny and Annabelle talk and laugh in front of us.

If only I could be with *them*!

But no, I'm still stuck with the *Girl of Doom*.

We trudge by the lake, which is on campus, and follow a trail into the woods. Even though I feel like *Gloomsville*, I have to admit, the woods are beautiful. We hop over fat twisted roots and tramp across wooden bridges. Birds warble in the trees, and frogs croak and plop into the marshes as we follow a winding path. It's a warm summery day, but the shade from the trees keeps us cool.

I can hear kids asking each other the let's-get-to-know-you questions. I have the list, but I haven't asked Melanie a single question.

When we stop for a snack, I pull out the questions. If we didn't *have* to fill in the answers, I wouldn't bother.

Ugh, here goes.

"Okay, Melanie, let's get this over with. What's your favorite family tradition?"

Melanie sighs and stares straight ahead.

"Backyard movies," she says. I fill in the blank.
That's actually one of *my* favorite family traditions
too, but I would never say that to Melanie. When
she asks me my favorite family tradition, I say,
"Making full-moon cookies." My family always bakes
cookies when there's a full moon.

"Pet peeves?" I ask. Melanie pinches a finger full of
trail mix from her snack bag and drops it into her
mouth.

"Bugs and bad hair days." I jot this down.

That's funny, I think. **Bugs are one of my pet peeves too, *especially* mosquitoes and spiders.** But I keep this information to myself too.

"Have you ever actually had a bad hair day?" I question. Melanie tilts her head toward me.

"*Everybody* has bad hair days, Heidi," she says like I'm ridiculous. "So what's *your* pet peeve?"

"**Mean girls,**" I say without hesitation. Melanie rolls her eyes and looks away. I probably shouldn't have said that. We were kind of getting along for a second.

"What one item can you *not* live without?" I ask.

I'm sure Melanie will say something annoying like lip gloss or fashion magazines.

But she doesn't.

"My phone," she says. *Well, that makes sense,* I think, remembering the other night when we had to turn in our phones. I should've guessed that one.

"I miss my phone too," I say. "But the one item I'm not sure I could live without would be gummy bears."

Melanie actually laughs. "Good one."

We answer the rest of the questions and discover that we have similar answers for everything.

Three words: *creepy* AND *surprising.*

But the last question is the hardest and scariest one of all.

"This one's a doozy," I say, preparing Melanie for what's about to come next. "What qualities would you like most in a broommate?"

Melanie drops her snack bag onto the ground.

She looks at me a little suspiciously. "Is that *really* the question?"

"Yup."

Melanie picks up her snack bag and gazes at the cattails in the marsh. "Okay, what I'd like most in a broommate is someone who's understanding, kind, and FUN. Guess *that's* not gonna happen."

I roll my eyes. "I think I'm lots of fun," I say. "But did you ever stop to think that I might like those same qualities in a broommate?"

Melanie looks away. Sometimes I wonder if she has a nice bone in her body.

We finish the hike, and Jenna tells us we walked FOUR miles. Wow, that's *so* far! And Melanie never complained once. I thought the wilderness would freak her out, but she was totally into it. I guess Little Miss Frou-Frou likes the great outdoors.

Shock-a-roon-i!

But that doesn't mean I like her. *As if.*

When we get back to campus, we have another outdoor picnic, like we did yesterday. Our next activity requires bathing suits, which is okay with me because it's gotten really hot outside. After we change, Jenna tells everyone to stand opposite their broommate.

"This game is called Cheese Head," Jenna explains as she hands out shower caps. Seriously? Wait, we have to wear shower caps in front of everybody? I don't even feel comfortable wearing a shower cap in front of my own family!

One word: *mortifying.*

And surprisingly, Melanie doesn't seem to mind the shower cap.

Another word: *unexpected.*

We tuck our hair inside the shower caps and take turns squirting canned whipped cream on top of each other's heads.

This is really FUN.

Jenna passes out bags of cheese puffs to each team. Melanie goes first. Whichever team gets the most cheese puffs to stick to their heads, wins. Jenna blows the whistle, and cheese puffs fly.

Melanie flings a cheese puff at my head. She's only allowed to throw one cheese puff at a time. Most of them hit me in the face.

Melanie and I giggle. It's hard not to.

"Shoot HIGHER!" I say, because naturally I want me and Melanie to win. Melanie tosses the cheese puffs

higher. Now they begin to land on my whipped-
cream-covered head.

"Okay, now everybody switch!" Jenna shouts.
Melanie hands me the bag of cheese puffs. I lob
them one by one onto Melanie's head. I have to
admit, it's harder than it looks. When I hit Melanie in
the face, we break into giggles all over again. She
doesn't even get mad.

Also unexpected.

Jenna blows the whistle and counts the cheese puffs on top of every team's heads. Then she announces the winners.

"The Cheese Head prize goes to Heidi Heckelbeck and Melanie Maplethorpe!"

Melanie and I turn to each other and high-five.

When we realize we're getting along, we back away, like, what was *that* all about?

Could I have been wrong about Melanie? Could she actually be . . . fun?

Then it's time for the slippery slide event. There are ginormous plastic sheets covering a hillside. The object of *this* game is to collect as many foam balls as you can as you slide down the hill. At the same time, kids and teachers spray you with water and shaving cream as you slide. We have to wear goggles so we don't get shaving cream in our eyes.

Melanie and I will race against Sunny and Annabelle, who are on the two slides next to us.

"Sliders, take your marks!" Jenna shouts. We kneel in front of the slides. "Get set! Go!" Melanie and I flop onto our stomachs and whiz down two slides. Foam balls, water, and shaving cream bombard us. I'm sliding so fast, I can't grab a single ball, but Melanie grabs two. Sunny and Annabelle snag a total of three.

"Heidi!" Melanie shouts at the bottom. "Would you at least TRY?"

As soon as Melanie yells at me, I feel the old anger rise up again. I can't help it, but I react with magic.

I make one of the cans of shaving cream start spraying Melanie relentlessly.

Melanie screams and runs up the hill. To someone
who doesn't know there are witches in the world, it
would look like the can had built up pressure inside
and just started spraying all by itself. But it is kind
of a reckless move, even for me.

Then it's our turn again. This time I'm going to focus on grabbing foam balls no matter what. I don't want to get yelled at again, but I don't want to lose either.

I'm focused and fierce.

This time I grab *two* balls. Melanie gets two as well.

"That's more like it!" Melanie says, and we bump fists. After every team finishes five runs, Jenna announces the winners.

"Heidi and Melanie win AGAIN!"

Melanie and I squeal, and everybody sprays us with shaving cream. And you know what's incredible? Even though I've known Melanie most of my life, I never knew she was athletic. She always acted prissy and perfect in elementary school.

My eyes are definitely being opened to new sides of Melanie.

Our prizes are party packs of lip gloss! *Woo!*

After that we get to play on the slides for fun. Hunter McCutie playfully throws foam balls at me.

Does that mean he LIKES me? I wonder.

Well, maybe not LIKE-like because he also chucks some balls at Melanie.

All I can say is, **he'd better not like HER.**

Jenna takes pictures of everyone before we get changed.

"Smile!" she shouts. Melanie and I stick out our tongues and do silly poses. I have to confess, it's been a fun day so far. But a little fun isn't going to erase years of hostility with Melanie.

After we shower and change, we have a cookout with s'mores.

My favorite.

Then we have one last activity, called Banana SPLIT. Jenna explains that everyone has to perform SURGERY on a BANANA. The team that finishes first wins.

What?!

At each station there are surgical gowns, skullcaps, masks, and surgical gloves. We also get a banana, a plastic knife, toothpicks, string, a plastic sewing needle, rubber bands, and tape. Melanie and I stand across from each other, and Sunny and Annabelle are next to us. We dress in our surgical outfits.

Then we attend to our patients, aka the bananas.

LOL!

I hold the knife over our banana and carve an
incision down the middle. Then I carefully remove
the fruit inside without breaking it. Next Jenna tells
us to cut the banana into five pieces.

"Now use your tools to put the bananas back
together," she instructs. "Can you make the banana
as good as it was before?"

I love this game. It makes me feel like a real surgeon.

Melanie is into it too.

We use toothpicks to put the banana back together.
The banana parts don't line up perfectly, so we
have to twist them to make it like it was before.
Then I tuck the mended banana back into the peel.

We carefully take turns sewing the incision on the banana peel. Melanie and I finish and ding the bell on the table.

Jenna comes over and inspects our *all-better* bananas.

"Looks like we have a winning team!" Jenna announces. This time we each get a gift card to the bookstore.

Normally I never win *anything*, but today Melanie and I won *everything*.

"Way to go!" Sunny says. Her banana is still in surgery with no hope of recovery. Then she whispers into my ear. "Melanie's not all that bad, Heidi. You two made an incredible team."

I have to admit, we *did* make a good team, but that still doesn't change the awful history between us.

Melanie and I walk back to the dorms with Sunny and Annabelle. I can't stop yawning—same with Melanie. Our lack of sleep has finally caught up with us. We say good night to Sunny and Annabelle and head toward Baileywick. Melanie turns and faces me.

Cheerful, happy Melanie is gone.

Cranky Melanie the doommate returns.

"Heidi, just because we won everything today doesn't mean I *like* you," she says.

Does Melanie *ever* take a day off from being mean to me?

Two words: *obviously, NO!*

"Gee, thanks for the reminder," I say.

All the good feelings from the day are suddenly gone.

Why does Melanie have to always be so mean?

Why can't she be nice for one whole day?

When we get to the dorm, Mrs. Kettledrum is waiting by the door. "Heidi, I need to speak with you."

I stop, and Melanie keeps walking.

Uh-oh, I think.

Why does my housemother want to speak with me?

I follow her to her apartment, and she asks me to sit down.

I take a seat on an old sofa that sinks when I sit. I wish it would swallow me up as I look at the stern expression on Mrs. Kettledrum's face.

"Heidi, it's come to my attention that you used magic both last night and during today's games. Is this true?"

I tuck a strand of hair behind my ear and think two things.

One: Mrs. Kettledrum is a witch.

And two: I'm *busted*.

"Yes, it's true," I confess, because somehow she already knows. Mrs. Kettledrum leans back on the couch.

"And would you please share with me *why* you used magic when you know that using it is highly discouraged outside certain classes?" Mrs. Kettledrum doesn't seem mad—just concerned.

I decide to tell her the truth.

First I apologize for breaking the rule. Then I tell her the story of how Melanie and I have never gotten along.

"So may I *please* have a different broommate?" I beg at the end of my story. "Melanie doesn't want to live with *me* any more than I want to live with *her*. We're totally incompatible."

Mrs. Kettledrum chuckles. "So I've heard," she says. "But, Heidi, you and Melanie were put together for a reason. The questionnaires you filled out last spring showed that you two have so much in common."

I hang my head, and Mrs. Kettledrum pats my shoulder. "Don't be discouraged, Heidi. Think about how well you two worked together today on Broommate Bonding Day. **You and Melanie stole the show!**"

"I know, but we still don't like each other," I remind my housemother. "We never have."

Mrs. Kettledrum laughs, like an old sage. "You may not believe this right now, but if you two learn to get along, it will help you both."

Then she puts her hands on her knees and stands up. "So, Heidi, I'm not going to report this to your family or give you a bad mark for using magic *this* time, but don't do it again or you could face the consequences. For now I only ask that you and Melanie learn to get along."

My shoulders fall with the weight of the verdict.

This is much WORSE than a bad mark on my record, I think.

And somehow I don't think I'll ever be free of Melanie.

I'm pretty sure I'm cursed.

SHOCK-A-ROO!

But then again, maybe I'm not.

When I get back to the room, Melanie's suitcases are packed.

"Did you get a room transfer?" I question.

She looks at me from the full-length mirror. "I'm asking for one tomorrow."

"Good luck with THAT," I say as I walk past her into the bathroom.

Maybe Melanie will have more success asking for a new broommate than I did. She's persuasive, **and, of course, she knows *all the right people*.**

Right now I'm too tired to care.

I brush my teeth and put on my pajamas. I scuff across the floor in my slippers, climb into bed, and switch off the light.

Melanie's already in bed, and tonight she skipped her headphones.

Thank goodness!

"Good night," I mutter, and I fall straight to sleep.

✧ ✧ ✧

The sun pricks my eyelids and wakes me up before Melanie's perfume or my alarm. It's the first day of classes and the first day of my School of Magic classes too.

I roll over and see Melanie's suitcases standing beside her bed.

I have to admit, in the light of day the sight of them actually makes me a little sad.

Even though we don't like each other, she *was* an amazing partner yesterday.

I still can't believe we won every event!

She's also from Brewster, which is pretty cool.

But still, I really wish I could have a broommate who's a witch, like me.

Melanie's definitely *not* a witch.

If Melanie *does* get a broommate transfer, who knows who'll move in.

Anybody is probably better than Melanie, right?

Then why do I feel so crummy?

After breakfast I go to English, math, science, and social studies. My teachers seem nice, and Melanie's not in ONE of my classes.

Not ONE!

Woo-hoo!

But for some reason she's still on my mind. I feel somewhat responsible for making her so miserable.

But *she* makes *me* miserable all the time too.

Ugh, and I know that doesn't make it right either.

That's when I decide to make a deal with myself:

Make up with Melanie whether she moves out or not.

I shouldn't stay mad at somebody I'm not even going to see every day anymore.

Wow, that decision made me feel better already!

At lunch Melanie sits on the opposite side of the table from me, so it's not a good time to talk.

I'm glad because all I can think about right now is my first School of Magic class. It's **right after lunch, and I'm so excited!**

I meet Sunny and Annabelle outside the cafeteria, and we head to class together.

The School of Magic is located in a hidden part of the school. All we've **been told is that the secret entrance is in the library.**

I guess nobody would suspect anything unusual to go on in the library.

"Have you cracked the STT code yet?" I ask Sunny as we walk over. She shakes her head.

"I'm trying to gain their trust, but so far no luck," Sunny says. "The minute I sat down at the table, I gave those kids a big smile and said, 'STT!' **They all looked at me like I was bananas.** One of them asked what I was talking about. But then I realized I shouldn't have said it so loud in the cafeteria. So I winked and said, 'Don't worry, your secret is safe with me!' Then they all shrugged and went back to their lunch."

"We know you'll figure it out," Annabelle says as we head inside. Ms. Egli greets us at the circulation desk.

She ushers us down a long hall and stops in front of a large grandfather clock with a moon and stars above the clock's face.

Ms. Egli asks for my library card. I unzip my backpack and fumble around for my card.

Found it!

"Heidi, wave your card in front of the keyhole," Ms. Egli tells me.

So I do as she says, and the door on the grandfather clock unlatches and opens partway.

Sunny, Annabelle, and I gasp.

"That's so cool!" I whisper.

Ms. Egli opens the door all the way, and we can see down a dimly lit tunnel.

"This is one of three entrances to the School of Magic," she says. "Each one can be accessed with your library card. One is behind the fountain in the courtyard. Simply hold your card over the fish's mouth, and a door will open. Then a long curvy slide will take you to your classrooms. The other entrance is in the basement of Baileywick and leads to an underground stone passageway."

Wow, a private entrance from my own dorm!

Cool perk!

"Ms. Egli, excuse me. I have a question," I say.

Ms. Egli nods at me. "Of course, Heidi," she says. "What is your question?"

"How have you been able to keep the School of Magic a secret for all these years?"

Ms. Egli smiles. "A very good—and very common—question," she answers. "The witches and wizards who work here put a harmless spell on every non-magical student on their move-in day.

"The spell makes it impossible for them to see witches or wizards enter the School of Magic.

"It also contains a key word, or trigger. If for any reason a non-magical student gets inquisitive and starts asking questions or tries to enter the School of Magic, Mrs. Kettledrum, Mr. Craftwood, or Ms. Charmsworth, or I will say the trigger word to the student, and they will immediately lose interest or forget they even asked about the School of Magic."

Sunny, Annabelle, and I look at one another. "Cool!" we all say at the same time.

"But even though there are spells protecting the School of Magic," Ms. Egli continues, leaning in close to the three of us, "all witches and wizards are still asked to refrain from using magic outside the School of Magic. It is important to take heed of this. For generations all of us—teachers, students, and alumni—have kept this magnificent and sacred school a secret. It's now up to you to take on this responsibility too."

Sunny, Annabelle, and I nod solemnly.

I've never seen Sunny look so serious, and suddenly I feel guilty for having already broken this rule.

I vow never to break it again.

"Okay, girls!" Ms. Egli says brightly. "Step inside the clock and follow the corridor into your new life. I promise, you're going to love it!"

I climb through the clock first and step down a few stairs into a wood-paneled corridor.

The only lights in the hallway emanate from picture frames on the walls. Each frame spotlights a portrait of an important witch or wizard alumnus.

Wow, I wonder if I'll earn a place on this wall someday.

All three of us squeal with excitement as we walk down the corridor. We have no idea what to expect on the other end.

Alumni witches and wizards are forbidden to reveal what's inside the School of Magic. They can only share general things about the classes, but nothing about what it looks like or what we might learn. Even my mom and Aunt Trudy haven't told me much.

At the end of the corridor is an arched door with cast-iron hinges.

"Go ahead, Heidi. Open it," Sunny whispers.

I look at my two friends and bite my lip with excitement. "Here goes . . . !"

I lift the iron latch and pull open the door. The main room is enormous and round, with a domed ceiling.

It feels like a room where important things happen.

Mystical symbols are painted on the ceiling, like a crescent moon, a compass, a pineapple, and a tree of life. The floor beneath the domed ceiling is marble with a spiral pattern. At the center of the spiral—in the middle of the room—is an eye. The entire spiral is enclosed by an outer circle in a different shade of marble. On one side of the room, **water cascades down an entire wall.** Off the main room in every direction are classrooms, labs, a café called Toil and Trouble, and Twinkles Book Shop.

"**It's like another whole world!**" I say.

"**Yeah, but it feels like home,**" Sunny adds.

"It should. This is our witch heritage and future," Annabelle adds. Other students, aka witches and wizards, file into the room. I recognize a few faces from orientation.

"Wow, for the first time in my life I don't feel like the lone witch at school," I say.

"Agreed," Sunny says.

"Same," Annabelle says. "And it feels *good*."

Shoes click across the marble floor as three
teachers walk to the center of the spiral. They have
on pointed hats and black robes. Aunt Trudy told me
these are only worn on special occasions. One of
the teachers is Mrs. Kettledrum.

"Everybody, please take a seat around the outside
edge of the circle," Mrs. Kettledrum says. Sunny,
Annabelle, and I sit down and crisscross our legs.

That's when I spy **Hunter McCutie.**

AHHH! He must be a WIZARD!

This is so exciting! He catches my eye and waves. I wave back. Sunny nudges me. My face heats up, so I look at the door. Nobody has come in for a while. Maybe everyone is here. *Nope!* Another girl just walked in, but it's not just any girl. I grab Sunny's knee with one hand and Annabelle's knee with the other.

"LOOK!" I panic-whisper. Sunny and Annabelle follow my eyes, and then they see what I see.

The girl who just walked in is *Melanie Maplethorpe.*

"Melanie's a WITCH?"

I'm 100 percent stunned.

"Looks like it," Sunny says.

"What a plot twist!" Annabelle adds.

I can't stop shaking my head.

"Sunny, please pinch me! I think I'm in a nightmare."

Sunny pinches my arm, and as I suspect, I'm very much awake.

I would have sooner believed my stuffed animals could talk than believe that Melanie Maplethorpe is a witch.

Melanie sees me and walks over. Her hands are on her hips.

"Heidi Heckelbeck! YOU'RE a WITCH?"

Somewhere in my shock, I find the muscles to nod my head.

Melanie looks as shocked as I feel.

We stare at each other as if for the first time. Neither of us can find words to express the mental jolt we've just experienced—*that is*, until Mrs. Kettledrum tells Melanie to take a seat.

Melanie walks across the room and sits down.

Wow, maybe there's more to Melanie's story than I know?

And I'm not entirely sure how I feel about Melanie being a witch. It's too unexpected and downright shocking.

How did I not know?

"Let's begin," Mrs. Kettledrum says, snapping me out of my thoughts. She welcomes everybody and then has the teachers introduce themselves.

Besides Mrs. Kettledrum, there's Mr. Craftwood and Ms. Charmsworth. I'm doing my best to listen, but my thoughts are reeling.

Were there any signs in elementary school that Melanie was a witch?

I can't think of any, except maybe that time she dressed as a witch for Halloween in second grade. I'll have to ask her about that.

Did she know then, or was that just a coincidence?

At least now I know how she was able to match my pranks the other night.

This is absolutely unbelievable.

Sunny nudges me to pay attention. I sit up straight.

Mr. Craftwood asks us to hold hands with the person on either side of us. Everyone clutches hands.

At that moment I wish I was sitting next to Hunter. 💚 💚

"This is called the Magic Circle," Mr. Craftwood explains. He has shoulder-length black hair and green eyes. He has jeans on underneath his Broomsfield robe. "Each day before training we'll gather here to form our Magic Circle."

"When we hold hands, it unifies us, and we become a force for good," says Mrs. Kettledrum, taking the lead. "This circle is a symbol of safety, protection, and love. Together we will learn to harness our wills and emotions to practice magic for the greater good. We'll also learn to protect ourselves from harmful influences. Today you officially become a part of a bigger family."

Mrs. Kettledrum stays in the middle of the circle. Ms. Charmsworth hands her a woven basket that looks a lot like the one Mrs. Kettledrum used to collect our cell phones. Mr. Craftwood lights a circle of candles around Mrs. Kettledrum.

"And now it's time for the Feather-Picking Ceremony," Mrs. Kettledrum announces.

"Each one of you will pick a feather. The color of your feather will reveal something unique about each one of you as a witch or wizard. When I call your name, please come forward and select a feather."

One by one Mrs. Kettledrum calls names. She holds the basket just high enough so no one can peek inside. Before each student picks a feather, Ms. Charmsworth chants this verse:

COME FORWARD NOW AND SELECT YOUR FEATHER.
WITCHES AND WIZARDS MUST BOND TOGETHER.
SHORE UP YOUR WEAKNESSES,
STRENGTHEN YOUR POWER.
THEN YOU'LL GROW STRONGER
WITH EACH PASSING HOUR.

After a feather is selected, Mr. Craftwood explains what the color of the feather means.

Soon it's *my* turn.

This is the moment I've been waiting for my entire life, I think.

I hope my feather reveals something wonderful!

"Heidi Helena Heckelbeck."

My heart races with anticipation as I walk toward Mrs. Kettledrum.

What color feather will I pick?

I hope it's a rainbow feather.

I tiptoe to reach into the basket, and then I pull out my feather.

It's gray.

No, not GRAY!

Gray is fine for clothes and bedspreads, **but not my important feather!**

Gray is the color of a cloudy day.

Gray is the color of wet cement.

Gray is gloomy.

Gray is depressing.

Gray isn't even a color!

Then Mr. Craftwood begins to describe my feather choice.

"Gray is the *balance* between light and darkness. Gray is the balance between two opposing forces. The one who selects the gray feather is uncommonly blessed with magic. With discipline, guidance, and perseverance, you will learn to find magical solutions to your own problems as well as others'."

I look at my gray feather with new interest.

It may be blah, but I love what it symbolizes.

Think of it!

I'm *uncommonly* blessed with magic!

Although I still have no idea what my special gift as a witch is, perhaps this is a sign of big things to come.

Sunny picks a bright yellow feather, of course. Her feather symbolizes the sun, which gives strength, joy, and light to the world.

That's *definitely* Sunny.

Annabelle picks a green feather, which symbolizes nature and healing.

Spot on!

Melanie picks a pink feather—no surprise there. Pink symbolizes beauty, courage, and kindness.

Courage and kindness? Do I even know Melanie? I wonder.

Then Hunter McCutie picks a black feather. The black feather symbolizes power and the ability to keep evil away.

So he's cute and *awesome,* I think.

Swoon.

After the ceremony the teachers split us up into four groups. I count twenty-four witches and wizards in our class.

Sunny and Annabelle are in my group. Yay!

Mrs. Kettledrum is our leader.

Melanie is in Hunter's group.

Boo! Hiss! Whatever!

Then we tour our magical new campus. Our first stop is the spells and potions classroom.

There's a cauldron at every station.

How cool is THAT?

The classroom for the science of herbs is inside a greenhouse. The entire ceiling is glass so the plants and herbs can grow.

On one side of the greenhouse—set away from all the plants—is a colorful collection of gems and crystal balls.

Next we visit the broom closet, which is more like a humongous gymnasium with extra-high ceilings.

In the middle is a gigantic mushroom—*not a real one*—and hanging from the mushroom cap are long chains.

At the end of each chain is a broomstick.

This is where we'll learn to ride broomsticks!

Mom and Aunt Trudy don't ever ride broomsticks. They say it's a little outdated and sometimes interferes with the space program.

Witches and wizards on brooms also make up a big portion of reported UFO sightings.

But who cares? It'll be FUN!

There's a magical creature workshop, but we're not allowed to see the magical creatures today.

Another classroom has a lake and a forest *inside* it.

Now, *that's* magical!

And then there's a classroom that has a wishing well in the middle of it, but we don't have time to go in.

"How do you keep all of this a secret from the other students?" one of the boys in my group asks.

Mrs. Kettledrum tells us more about what Ms. Egli told me, Sunny, and Annabelle in the library. The teachers use invisibility and protection spells to mask everything.

Then Mrs. Kettledrum shows us the other entrances into the School of Magic.

The entrance from Baileywick is an old coal chute that leads to an underground tunnel, lighted by electric torches.

The entrance by the fountain is my favorite because it has the swirly slide. All you have to do is sit on the slide, and it takes you right to the secret classrooms.

Broomsfield Academy is the most magical place I've ever been, not including the magical library in Brewster.

The tour takes up the rest of the double period.

Next week we'll start our magic lessons, but now it's the end of the day.

Time for dinner.

I know I'm going to love it here, but I still have the Melanie problem, I think as I walk back to the dorms with Sunny and Annabelle.

One thing Mrs. Kettledrum told us was, "in order to practice magic effectively, you have to empty your mind of bad thoughts."

This stood out to me because I've had nothing *but* bad thoughts about Melanie since second grade.

Then I picked a gray feather.

Gray means I'm the balance between two opposing forces.

Melanie and I are definitely two opposing forces.

But how am I supposed to be the balance? I wonder.

The answer is both easy and really hard.

I have to let go of our rivalry.

The only thing it does is make us *both* miserable.

And over the past few days, I've realized that Melanie and I have a lot more in common than I thought.

We're both competitive.

We both have a good sense of humor.

And we're both strong-willed.

And, come to find out, we're both witches!

Okay, it's time for me to deal with this. Melanie and I *have* to talk this out.

And no matter how hard it might be, I also *have* to let go of this rivalry for both of us.

I really hope I can do it!

This may not be magic, but I think it's a step in the right direction.

COMMON GROUND

When I get back to our room, Melanie's on her bed, propped against her fuzzy pink backrest. Her suitcases are now parked beside the door. *Am I too late?* I wonder as I walk toward my bed.

"So *did* you get a room transfer?" I ask, because that's the only place I can think of to start the conversation and, well, I kind of want to know too. Melanie turns her head toward the window and then looks back at me.

"No," she says. "They wouldn't let me. I had a meeting with Principal Ray and Mrs. Kettledrum this morning."

I sit on the edge of my bed and face Melanie. "They wouldn't let me transfer either," I say.

Then I gather my courage to ask my big question. "So, Melanie, I was wondering if you wanna *talk*?"

Melanie hoists her body higher on her backrest and sighs. "I don't know," she says. "We probably *should.*"

I look at my sneakers for a sec and then back at Melanie. "Well, let me start by saying, I can't BELIEVE you're a witch!"

A smile spreads across Melanie's face. She even laughs a little. "I can't believe YOU'RE a witch either! How come we never knew?"

I kick off my shoes and hop onto my bed. "I dunno," I say. "Maybe because we never gave each other a chance." This takes my mind right back to the first day of school at Brewster Elementary. "You know, Melanie, I've always wanted to ask you something. . . ."

"What?"

I take a deep breath. It's time for the question I've been wanting to ask her for sooo long.

Here goes nothing, I think, and then speak.

"Well, how come you were so mean to me on the first day I arrived at school in second grade?"

Melanie shrugs and looks away. I can tell she's searching her mind for reasons. "Who knows," she finally says. "When you first arrived, it felt like everything was going to change. Plus everybody liked you and that made me feel competitive."

I raise an eyebrow. "*I* made you feel *competitive*?"

Melanie nods. "Yeah, from the moment you walked in the door, it felt like we were rivals. You were so confident, and everyone just gravitated toward you. I guess I was jealous. I never gave you the chance to be my friend."

I prop up my pillows and lean against them. "When you said rude things to me or about me, well, it just made me mad. And by the way, you *still* pick on me."

Melanie's face turns pink, but she breaks into a sort of smile. "I know," she says. "It kind of turned into a bad habit. But you're not exactly nice to *me*, either."

I laugh. "Okay, fair enough. But what about *now*? Do you think we might be able to get along here?"

Melanie takes a deep breath and sighs again. "That's a good question," she says. "I think we're going to *have* to get along whether we like it or not."

We both laugh a little nervously.

This is definitely new territory for both of us.

"Well, I never would have expected it, but one thing I've learned over the last few days is that we actually have a lot in common," I say. "And you're a lot tougher than I thought too. I thought you'd hate going on a hike."

Melanie rolls her eyes. "I love the outdoors! Just because I wear cute clothes doesn't mean I don't like nature. But I get what you're saying. And you're right, we *do* have a lot in common.

"Who would have thought we had *anything* in common?"

I laugh. "I *know!* It's amazing! We were actually the *best* team on Broommate Bonding Day. I never knew you were so athletic."

Melanie's blue eyes light up. "I love sports!"

"And to top it off, we're *both* witches!" I repeat because I still can't believe it. "You're the pretty witch, and I'm the girl-next-door witch."

Melanie blushes. "Actually, Heidi, you're pretty too," she says. And I cough because I'm so shocked to hear those words come out of Melanie's mouth.

"Okay, don't let it go to your head," she adds. "And by the way, I can totally help put your look over the top." She pauses for a sec. "If you want."

And these are honestly the nicest words that Melanie has *ever* said to me.

I can feel the animosity between us melting.

For real.

"Sure," I say. "I'm open to beauty tips, but I want to keep my own style too."

Melanie leans forward and wraps her arms around her knees. "Your look is pretty cool—even though I dis it sometimes. It may not be *my* look, but it doesn't mean it's a *bad* look."

Wait, did those words just come from the mouth of Melanie Maplethorpe too?

Wow, I never knew she could be so . . . *nice!*

"Thanks," I say. "Your look is very cool and totally posh, too. *So-o-o-o-o . . .*"

"So *what?*" Melanie asks.

"So do you actually wanna *be* broommates?"

Melanie leans back and crisscrosses her legs. "Like I said, I'm not sure we have a choice." And still there's no trace of snootiness in her tone, so that's good.

"I *know*, but do you want to be, like, *fun* broommates?" I press.

Melanie smiles. "Yeah," she says. "I'd *really* like that. But no more sand in my bed, and I promise not to put another tickle spell on you in the middle of the night. Mrs. Kettledrum totally busted me for that one."

I gasp.

"I got busted for using magic outside class too! I just can't figure out how they knew."

Melanie shrugs. "There are very skilled witches all over this school. Who knows what kind of alarms they've rigged to detect when magic is being used?"

"Good point," I tell her. And it really is.

I've been using magic for so long that it's like second nature, but I need to stop using it at Broomsfield unless I'm doing it for magic classes.

I don't want to get in trouble again, or worse, get kicked out of school.

I'm really starting to like it here. There's Sunny and Annabelle and Hunter and even Melanie.

And for the first time in my *whole* entire life, well at least since second grade, I have a new feeling around Melanie.

Warmth.

THE FIRST DAY OF THE REST OF MY LIFE

It's Friday! Woo!

I survived my first week of boarding school.

What a ride.

Three words: *I. Love. It.*

We got our phones back today too!

Only for the weekend, of course, but still.

Whew!

Melanie kisses her phone every five seconds, like it's some long-lost puppy.

Hilarious!

But I know it means more to her than that.

She confessed to me last night that when she arrived, she was *really* homesick . . . like, crying-into-her-pillow-every-night homesick.

When they took away her phone, she felt like she was totally cut off from her family and everything familiar, except me, which was less than ideal.

But everything is starting to fall into place now.

Melanie just unpacked her suitcases, so we're settling in all over again, but in a much better way this time.

Melanie is going home for the weekend, and I'm staying at school.

I'm afraid if I go home, it might make me homesick again, and I'm just beginning to get used to it here.

"Hey, Heidi, come here!" Melanie calls.

She's sitting at her desk in front of a makeup mirror that lights up. The mirror has various settings that create different shades of light. It also has a magnifying setting.

Seeing your face super-magnified is definitely not *MAG-nificent.*

Melanie runs across the room and drags my chair over to her desk.

"Sit!" she commands—in a fun way.

And, like a well-trained dog, I sit in the chair beside her. She pulls a spongy-tipped wand from a tube of lip gloss and holds it in front of my face.

"Mm-kay, now look at me."

I look at Melanie with wide eyes and brace myself for what comes next.

"Trust me," she says. "This lip gloss will give your lips EXPLOSIVE shine, and it has a little smidge of coral to give your lips some color, too. Perfect with your strawberry-blond hair."

She smears the spongy tip across my lips. Then she turns the mirror toward me.

My lips are super-shiny, and it *does* look nice, I'll admit, but . . .

"It feels like slug slime," I say.

Melanie throws her head back dramatically. "And how do you know what slug slime feels like?"

I shrug. "You're right. It feels more like unicorn snot."

Melanie whacks my shoulder playfully.

"That is SO GROSS! But I promise you'll get used to it after you use it a few times."

She dabs some blush onto my cheeks and rubs it in. "So have you noticed anyone *cute* in our class?"

Of course I have! I say to myself.

I can't stop the smile that sweeps across my face when I think of Hunter McCutie.

Melanie sees my face in the mirror and squeals.

"Oh my gosh! You're crushing, *aren't you*?! You can totally tell me, Heidi. I won't say a word, I promise!"

I dodge Melanie's eyes. I'm not ready to reveal my crush. It's too soon.

"Okay, if you won't tell me *yours*, then I'll tell you MINE," says Melanie. "There was this boy in my group the other day, and he's SO supercute. His name is Hunter McCann. Have you met him?"

I swear my stomach drops so far that it hits the floor.

Is she kidding me right now?! I say to myself, keeping a poker face on the outside.

Melanie canNOT like MY crush!

But SHE DOES! Ugh!

Why do Melanie and I ALWAYS clash, even when we're trying not to?

The old anger bubbles inside me, and I do a deep dive into the Land of Jealousy.

What's worse is that Hunter will probably like *Melanie* too because she's so pretty and perfect.

Okay, I'm officially depressed again.

But the worst thing I can do right now is let it ruin the friendship that is starting to form between me and Melanie . . . or let her know that I have the same crush.

"Yeah, I've met him," I say, trying to sound normal. "And he *is* really cute."

Melanie looks at me in the mirror. "I know, RIGHT?"

Her phone dings, and she checks it. "Oh, Heidi, I've gotta go! My parents are here. I'm SO excited! I can't wait to go home and see my pug, Lola. I miss her SO much."

Melanie grabs her overnight bag by the handle and looks at me. "I never thought I'd say this, but I think we'll be *awesome* broommates."

Some of my jealousy melts when she says this, and I shove the rest of it into a closet way in the back of my head. I can't start the *Melanie-Heidi Wars* all over again.

I hop up from the chair and give Melanie a hug.

"We've come a long way this week, and I think we'll be awesome broommates too," I say, but a tiny part of my brain is not 100 percent committed to what my mouth just said.

Melanie smiles. "Have a great weekend, Heidi."

"I will. You too. By the way, I meant to ask you earlier, what's your special gift as a witch?"

Melanie brings her wrist to her nose and sniffs it.

"Potions," she says. "I'm a total brew chick! I have a gift for mixing incredible scents, and I want to make life-changing, cruelty-free beauty products. Always have . . . that's actually how I first discovered I was a witch. I'll have to tell you about it when I get back. What about you?"

I should've known that beauty potions would be Melanie's special gift as a witch.

It's *sooo* obvious.

"That's really cool. My aunt Trudy is gifted at potions too. She has a mail-order perfume business. I'm still figuring out what my gift might be."

Melanie rolls her overnight bag to the door.

"It'll come," she says—just like everyone else has said to me this week. "See ya!"

"See ya!"

I listen to Melanie's bag wheel down the hallway.

Now that she's gone, I wonder what I should do?

I know! I'll check my mailbox.

Maybe Aunt Trudy wrote back to me.

I grab my room key, jog over to the mail room, and ask the clerk if I have any mail.

"Did you get an email?" the clerk asks. "We send one whenever you receive anything."

I shake my head. "No, but I'm pretty sure I have mail. My name is Heidi Heckelbeck."

The clerk walks to the back and after what seems, like, FOREVER, he returns with a letter AND a package.

JACKPOT!

I run all the way back to my room with my loot.

I don't even stop at Honeysuckle to say hi to Sunny and Annabelle.

Maybe later.

I haven't gotten *real* mail since I was at summer camp, so this is **super-exciting**.

As soon as I get to my room, I grab a pair of scissors and snip open my package. It's full of pink-and-white polka-dot tissue paper. There's a card on top. I tear it open. It has a kitten looking at the moon and stars and says, *I love you to the moon and back*!

And there's a letter from Lucy— my BFF!

Lucy

Dear Heidi,
Heyyyyy! How are you?!!! It's been a long, totally miserable week without you. Miss you sooo much. You left a humongous hole in my life! No guilt intended.
This week Bruce and I made rock

candy in his lab. It was all very scientific—you know Bruce—and also delicious! You would've loved it.
I met a new girl in homeroom named Molly Meadows. She's nice, but not nearly as hilarious as you. I haven't seen Melanie once. We're not in any classes together. *Phew!*
So when are you coming home? I need a Heidi fix!
Hope you like school—only that's kind of a lie because I secretly wish you don't so you'll come home. JK—only not really.
Miss you! Love you!

Your best friend,
Lulu, aka Loo-ney Tunes, aka Li'l Lu, aka Lulu Lemons, aka the Lucinator. *wink, wink!*
xoxo

P.S. Hope you like the treats!

Lucy is the absolute best,

I think as I gently pull back the tissue paper. Underneath I find a bag of gummy bears.

She knows they're my favorite,

which reminds me, I haven't touched the secret stash of GBs I brought to school.

And now I have MORE!

I tear into the bag and pop a red one into my mouth.

Chewy cherry bliss.

Then I dig deeper into the box and pull out a present. I tug on the white ribbon and unwrap it. It's a pair of black-and-white-striped socks that say "Love" on the bottom of one foot and "You" on the other.

So stinkin' CUTE.

Lucy's package makes me miss her and home so much.

I'm not sure which is harder—to be left behind or to leave?

They're both hard.

Then I open my letter from Aunt Trudy.

My dearest Heidi,
By the time you get this, I know things will
be better with Melanie.

I can only imagine how hard it was to find
out she is your roommate. Sometimes these
things happen for a reason. Rooming with
Melanie will make both of you grow in
wonderful ways. It may not always be easy,
but you'll discover she's not as bad as you think.

If she acts snooty or unkind, stand your
ground. See her bad behavior as an ugly
Halloween mask, and then look right
through it.

She doesn't have the power to make you feel
unsure of yourself unless you believe what
she says. <u>Don't believe it</u>. It's not true.

I miss you, my loving, kind, smart, beautiful, magical, and mischievous niece. If you want to talk more, I'll be home this weekend. Just give me a ring.

Thrilled to hear you're in Baileywick! I can picture you in that wonderful old dorm, and by now you've learned that it has a secret passageway to the School of Magic too. How fun is THAT?

Say hi to Mrs. Kettledrum for me. Your mom and I go way, way back with her. Someday I'll tell you all about the antics we got up to when the three of us were students at Broomsfield!

Loving you always,
Aunt Trudy
P.S. I didn't fall over when I heard the "bad" news. *Ha-ha!*

I fold the letter and slip it back into the envelope. Aunt Trudy's right. Things are so much better with Melanie, except for the annoying problem of us liking the same boy.

Ugh.

I decide to write Lucy back right away.

HEIDI HELENA HECKELBECK

Dear Luuuuucy!
I miss you so much! And your letter made me miss you even more. Thank you, thank you, thank you for the gummy bears and the socks! You really do know me better than anyone else! Sooo . . . there is a very good reason you haven't seen Melanie around.

She's here.

With me.

She's my ROOMMATE!
No, I am not kidding.

At first I thought it was the worst thing that could have ever happened. But the last few days have been surprising, to say the least. I'll tell you more about it when I see you in person, but Melanie may not be as bad as we thought she was.

(Again, I am NOT kidding!!!)

More to come when I see you.
Oh . . . and there's a boy.

Love you! Miss you!
Xoxoxoxoxoxoxoxo
Heidi
P.S. Send more gummy bears!!!!

I slide off my bed and decide to do my laundry. I have just enough time before dinner. Broomsfield has a laundry service, but I already know how to do my own.

I grab my detergent and dirty-clothes bag and head to the laundry room. I empty the bag into the washer, drop in a pod, and press start.

When I get back to my room, I have another gummy bear and reread my letters.

Then I shut my eyes and lean against my pillows.

I can't help it.

I miss home.

I don't want to leave boarding school, but I wish I could see my parents and Henry for just a little bit.

Being away from them makes me appreciate them more than ever and love and miss them *so* much.

I give a huge sigh as I head down to dinner.

I spot Sunny and Annabelle right away.

"Heidi, come sit with us!" Sunny says. I spot Jenna, and she smiles and waves and nods at me that it's okay to sit with my friends.

The minute I sit down, Sunny has some news.

"So I learned what 'STT' means," she says.

"I couldn't stand it anymore, so I asked one of the kids who first said it. She said at home, when her mom cooks, she makes everything very bland—no salt, no sugar, no seasonings. She thinks it's easier because then everybody can add whatever spices they want.

"'STT' means 'season to taste,' the girl said.

"So when she tasted the cafeteria food and it was very bland, she told her friends it was cooked the same way as her mom cooked—STT. Season to taste!"

Sunny covers her face with her hands for a moment.

"I felt so silly for thinking it was a mysterious witch code," she says. "Of course I didn't tell them what I thought it could have been, but they were all really nice when they explained what it meant."

Annabelle and I both laugh with Sunny. I'm glad the kids were nice and weren't mean to her.

Tonight's dinner is turkey meat loaf, mashed potatoes, string beans, and sweet corn.

"Those kids were right. This food is totally STT," Annabelle says.

She grabs the salt and sprinkles a little over her food.

We can't help but all giggle again about the STT misunderstanding.

I don't mind meat loaf that much, but **it makes me homesick again because I know Henry hates it.** I can just picture him arguing with my mom, trying to get out of eating it, and I smile.

"Why does it have to be turkey meat loaf?" I hear Sunny say. **"Why can't they just serve turkey burgers instead? It's pretty much the same thing, when you think about it."**

I look up and nod. "Totally," I say to Sunny. "Good point."

Sunny looks confused.

"What's a good point?"

"That turkey meat loaf and turkey burgers are pretty much the same thing. You just said that, right?"

Sunny and Annabelle look at each other.

"Nooooo," Sunny says slowly. "I didn't *say* that."
She pauses. "But I did just *think* that!"

I still don't get it. "What do you mean you just
thought that?"

Annabelle squeals. "Heidi, don't you get it?

"YOU JUST READ SUNNY'S MIND!"

I gasp.

"Th-that's not possible," I stammer.

"I've never been able to do that.

"Ever."

Annabelle squeezes her eyes shut.

"Heidi, do me now! Tell me what I'm
thinking!"

I concentrate as hard as I can, but I come up empty.

"I'm sorry," I say. "It must have been a onetime, fluky thing."

I look over at Sunny, who is smiling at me, her eyes sparkling. She's not saying a word, but I still hear her voice saying, *Heidi, if you can*

hear what I'm thinking right now, howl like a wolf!

I laugh and look at both my friends.

Then I shut my eyes and say, **"Ahh-wooo!!!"**

A few people around the cafeteria look at us, but we're too busy giggling to care.

I look at Sunny and say, "I'm not really sure how a wolf howls."

"Close enough!" Sunny says.

"Did you ask Heidi to howl like a wolf—with your mind?" Annabelle asks.

"I did!" Sunny says.

"And I howled!" I say proudly.

"This is so exciting," Annabelle says. "It must be your special power! I wonder why you can't read my mind, though."

Sunny takes a bite of meat loaf and chews thoughtfully. "I've known Heidi longer than you," she says. "Maybe that's why my thoughts come to her more easily.

"But I bet as time goes on, your power will get stronger and stronger.

"Someday you might be able to read EVERYBODY'S mind, Heidi!"

My head starts to spin.

It's more than I ever imagined possible.

"I need to process this," I tell them. "For now can we just eat our meat loaf and talk about something else?"

Sunny and Annabelle nod. Annabelle starts talking about a cute sweatshirt she saw in the campus store. "I don't usually like sweatshirts, but this one is on sale, and it's the prettiest shade of . . ."

As she's speaking, I hear Sunny's voice again.

I know you don't want to talk about this now, Heidi, but don't let it scare you. I think it's supercool.

Okay, okay! I'll stop sending you thoughts now.

I give Sunny a quick grateful glance, and she smiles.

After dinner and before I go to sleep, I have a video call with my parents.

It feels so good to talk to them.

I can hear Henry chattering in the background as I tell my mom **what I learned about myself tonight.**

My mom goes quiet, and I hear what she is thinking.

Telepathy, I hear her think through the phone.

Heidi, that's your special gift!

I can't believe I can hear my mom's thoughts too—and through the phone!

"Telepathy?" I blurt out. "What's that?"

"It's a fancy word that means you can communicate with just your mind," Mom replies.

"I don't know if I can communicate," I say. "So far I've only heard Sunny's thoughts and your thoughts just now."

"Your powers will get stronger as time goes on, Heidi," Mom says. "I've known other witches with this power.

"You'll start to be able to hear people's thoughts if you want to.

"And then maybe someday you'll be able to send your thoughts to people without saying anything too!"

"But I don't even know how I did it," I say.

"And I definitely have no idea how to do it again."

"That's okay. You don't have to know everything today," Mom says.

"You'll learn how to hone your telepathy skills at school, and your instructors will teach you how to use them safely and responsibly."

Dad coughs and looks at Mom.

"I don't know if I like the idea of Heidi knowing my thoughts," he says. "If nothing else, it will make holidays a lot less fun."

Dad has a point. No more surprise holiday or birthday gifts!

And I LOVE surprises!

Mom smiles.

"You'll learn ways to turn off your powers for a while when you want to, Heidi.

"And more experienced witches and wizards have ways to block your powers too."

"Really?" I say.

I hadn't thought about that.

Mom nods. "Your instructors need to be able to teach you without you reading their thoughts. And vice versa.

"Any teachers who might also be

telepathic don't need to read your thoughts about having lunch with your friends."

"Wow. This is soooo much to think about," I say.

I must look worried, because my dad speaks up again.

He might not be magical, but he always knows the right thing to say.

"We are all here for you, Heidi," he says.

I can feel tears of relief, excitement, and love for my family well up behind my eyes.

"Thank you," I tell my parents.

"This is certainly going to be an interesting year."

We hang up not long after, promising to chat again tomorrow.

I'm suddenly very tired.

It has been quite a week.

And I hate to admit it, but I'm a little lonely without Melanie here.

I'm looking forward to her return on Sunday night.

I turn out the light, snuggle under the covers, and let my mind settle.

A feeling of contentment and happiness washes over me.

And then I smile.

So, everything might still be confusing,

and there's so much I don't know about what the year will bring

and what my powers mean,

but my life as a witch . . .

and at Broomsfield Academy . . .

is just beginning.

I know it's going to be challenging,

and some days might even be really hard,

but it is also going to be FUN!

Here we go!

DREAM BOY

Little-known fact about me:

I absolutely love it when I wake up before my alarm.

It means one beautiful thing: *lounging in bed*!

Right now I have a whole half hour to luxuriate in my cool, crisp sheets while I listen to the birds sing, chirp, and call outside my window.

And best of all, I have time to think about the biggest, most important thing in the whole wide world right now—

my crush!!

I've been thinking about him basically nonstop since my first day at Broomsfield Academy.

His name is Hunter McCann.

But I secretly call him Hunter McCutie.

I really like, like, *like* him!

I point my toes and swish my legs back and forth excitedly under the covers.

Eeeee! I squeal inside my head. What if my crush turned into my boyfriend?

I am positively bursting with anticipation. Ever since I first saw Hunter, I've had a nonstop Fourth of July sparkler going off inside me.

Sizzle! Pop! Hiss!

It's like my whole being is filled with fizzing, popping heart-shaped candy!

Yup, I've got it BAD.

Okay, so how would I describe my dream boy, aka Hunter McCutie? Hmmm, let's see. Well, he's . . .

SuperCUTE!

Positively ADORABLE!

Chatty in a good way!

Deliciously drool worthy!

Totally hilarious!

Bewitchingly magical, as in he is a *wizard*!

Fun to be around.

Rocks a cool beachy style.

Strong and athletic.

And did I mention he's SO
SUPERCUTE?!

Hunter is from California and has that effortless endless-summer surfer look, with honey-colored bangs, freckles, and a swagger that is always ON.

The best part of all is that I think he likes me too. Or at least I hope so! Because he's sweeter than sweet, and I know we'd make the perfect couple.

Wow, I can just imagine our picture in the yearbook. Hearts EVERYWHERE . . . !

Zeeeep!

Zeeeep!

Zeeeep!

Aack!

That horrifying sound is my alarm clock, and it just popped my beautiful daydream like a cat claw in a balloon.

I had to buy an alarm clock for boarding school because we're not allowed to have our phones during the week.

"Heidi, please turn that killer-bee buzzing sound OFF!"

That's my roommate, Melanie Maplethorpe, **who is my former BEF (best enemy forever).** She's also from my hometown of Brewster.

We got the shock of our lives when we moved into Broomsfield Academy **only to discover that we were roommates—or rather** *broommates.*

What were the chances of THAT happening?

If that isn't incredible enough, I also found out that Melanie's a witch, like me!

And there's MORE madness to this story!

Melanie and I learned that we actually have a lot in common, so now we're kinda, sorta *friends*.

We're not *best* friends, like Lucy Lancaster and me, but I think it's safe to say we're *friends in progress*.

Wham! I hit the button on my alarm.

Then Melanie's alarm goes off.

Bling-a-ling-a-ling!

Bling-a-ling-a-ling!

Melanie has a retro pink alarm clock with two silver bells on top. She whacks it with her hand, and the room goes quiet for a blissful second.

Then Melanie throws back her covers, rubs her eyes, and slides into her pink fuzzy slippers.

Whisp! Whisp! Whisp!

I hear her slippers scuff into the bathroom. She's always the first one up. I'm the lounger.

As I lie in bed, I think about what to wear. Now that it's full-on fall, it's a little chilly, so I'm going to wear my new sweater. It has wide sage-green stripes, thin black stripes, and medium-wide cream stripes. I'll wear it with black leggings and a matching green headband. *Done!*

Then I roll over and—*oops!*—fall back to sleep. *Zzzzzzzzzz.*

I wake up in a panic. Melanie's long gone, but her flowery-fruity perfume lingers. I look at my clock. *Oh no! I only have twenty minutes to get ready and go to class! Eeek!*

I leap out of bed and summon my outfit with magic. The outfit flies from my drawers and onto my bed. I'm not supposed to use magic outside class unless it's for homework, **but I simply must use it right now or I'll be totally late!**

My clothes follow me into the bathroom. I splash my face with water, dress, and push my hair back with my headband. I give myself a quick magical manicure: French tips today. Then I fan my fingers and admire my work. So cute!

Okay, gotta go! I grab my backpack and zip down the sidewalk to the Barn—that's where the cafeteria is. I don't have time for breakfast, but I do have a few seconds to spare to check the seating assignments. Each student is assigned new classmates to sit with every so often. It's a great way to get to know everyone in your grade. I always love to see who's at my table.

Maybe Hunter will be at my table this week.

Fingers crossed.

When I get to the cafeteria, everybody's leaving for class. I run my finger down the table assignments. I'm at Table 1, which is Jenna's table. She's the resident advisor in my dorm, and she's totally awesome.

I go down the list some more. Sunny and Annabelle are at my table!

Sunny and Annabelle are roommates. I met Sunny at the beach one summer, long before we came to Broomsfield Academy. I was so happy to see her on my first day here. She introduced me to Annabelle, and we all became fast friends. I'm so happy they'll be at my table.

And oh my gosh! Hunter McCutie is at my table too!! *Swoon!*

Then my heart totally deflates because Melanie is also at my table. It's not that I don't like her. It just stinks because she has a HUGE crush on Hunter too.

MERGS to that! I've had to keep my crush a secret from her, since we're crushing on the *same* guy. The last thing I want is for Melanie and me to slip back into despising each other again.

But how can I talk to Hunter with Melanie at the table? *Rats-a-roni!*

Melanie brushes by me on her way out of the cafeteria. She's talking to a girl named Isabelle Summer. Isabelle is captain of the girls' soccer team here at Broomsfield Academy. She has beautiful dark, curly hair and wears it in a high ponytail.

She's effortlessly pretty.

Melanie and Isabelle smile as they walk by. I smile back and dash to the cafeteria counter to grab a granola bar. I definitely don't need my stomach growling in class.

One word: *mortifying!*

As I race to class, I remember I have to pick a famous person to write about for social studies. It's called a luminaries report. A luminary is an inspiring person of brilliant achievement. There are so many famous people from history who inspire me. I'm having a lot of trouble deciding.

I'm pretty much lost in my thoughts when THIS happens. . . .

CLONK! I bonk into somebody.

Aaagh!

Then I look up. I've crashed right into Hunter!

Double aaagh!

Now I have a beet-red face to go with my red hair.

I wonder if there's a way to use magic to rewind this horrifying encounter!!!

But before I can figure that one out, I see Hunter's sparkling green eyes. His face crinkles with laughter. He's not mad at me or even annoyed. He thinks our sudden encounter is FUNNY!

"Wow, Heidi!" he says. "What planet are you on this morning? Are you okay?"

I laugh like a goofy cartoon character.

One word: *awkward.*

"Sorry, Hunter!" I manage to say. "I'm fine. I was thinking about my social studies assignment. Are you okay?"

He nods, and he's *still* laughing.

Maybe he thinks I'm funny!

Or maybe he's laughing AT me.

We both jump when the bell rings. I shift my backpack up on my shoulder. "We'd better run, or we'll be late for class!" I say.

Hunter and I take off.

He's wearing khaki shorts and a pink polo frayed at the hem. He totally puts the chic into his shabby-chic beach look. I **love it!**

"We can make it if we hurry!" he says.

I'm chasing Hunter McCutie across campus! It's weird and wonderful.

English hasn't started as we slide into our seats. *Phew!*

Note to self: write to Lucy and tell her I crashed into my crush.

It's SO hard to sit still in class. I feel like a Christmas tree that just got plugged in. Every part of me is blinking and swirling, and I'm trimmed with excitement. I tell myself to chill about a hundred times, but that's like telling a popcorn machine to stop popping.

Heidi, you're a calm, all-together middle schooler.

I WISH.

And why do I keep hearing Hunter's name over and over? *Hunter McCann. Hunter McCann. Hunter McCann.*

Am I losing my mind?

Nope. I'm not losing it, because it's not *my* voice!

I look around the room. That's weird. Nobody is talking, but I still hear the voice, and what's more, I *know* that voice.

Then it hits me. It's *Melanie's* voice!

I'm not used to hearing other people's thoughts yet. Reading minds is my gift as a witch. The only problem is that I just discovered my gift and I have no idea how it works. For example, I never know when I'll tune in to someone else's thoughts. It just happens. And it's happening right now!

And guess what Melanie's thinking about?

Hunter. Merg!!!

Why do we have to like the same person?!

I zoom in on her thoughts. Now that I know it's Melanie, her thoughts are coming in loud and clear.

She's staring at Hunter from across the room and thinking: *One day we'll get married!*

Seriously? I think. Melanie's thinking about marriage in middle school?

Okay, that's way over the top. I keep listening. . . .

And when we have children, they'll be so gorgeous. They'll probably be supermodels. Everyone will stop and stare!

I cough to get Melanie off her train of thought.

It's too much.

I feel a little sick to my stomach.

I can't wait to learn in my magic classes how to control my gift of being able to read minds. For now my coughing does the trick, and Melanie starts paying attention to the teacher.

My thoughts, on the other hand, start drifting away.

I wonder if Hunter and I like the same things?

Does he like mint-chocolate-chip ice cream like me?

Or the color blue?

Is his favorite animal a dolphin?

"Hei-i-i-di-e-e?" I hear a voice call my name from far, far away. "Heidi Heckelbeck? Would you care to join us?"

I come back to earth and look at my teacher, Ms. Langley. She laughs.

"Heidi, please turn to chapter six."

I flip through my book to find the right page. The pages slap loudly as everyone waits for me to catch up.

Someone snickers. Ever since I started having a crush, my head has been in outer space.

Since when did my favorite subject become *boys*?

Okay, make that one *certain* boy.

But the more pressing question is: How am I going to make this one certain boy like me? And what if he likes Melanie better?

I have so many things on my mind.

No wonder it feels like I'm floating in outer space!

ABOUT THE AUTHOR

Wanda Coven has always loved magic. When she was little, she used to make secret potions from smooshed shells and acorns. Then she would pretend to transport herself and her friends to enchanted places. Now she visits other worlds through writing. Wanda lives with her husband and son in Colorado Springs, Colorado. They have three cats: Hilda, Agnes, and Claw-dia.

ABOUT THE ILLUSTRATOR

Anna Abramskaya was born in Sevastopol, Ukraine. She graduated from Kharkiv State Academy of Design and Arts in 2006. Then she moved to the United States, where she's currently living in the beautiful city of Jacksonville, Florida. Anna has loved art since she was little and has tried different materials and techniques. The process of creation and seeing beauty in the simple things around her always brings her joy and the wish to share that feeling with everyone. Anna wants to believe that art can help bring more love into people's hearts. Find out more at AnnaAbramskaya.com.